IO153387

ISBN: 978-1-945469-02-2
Cover Design: Jenna Hill
Book Layout: Jenna Hill
Front Cover Photos: Jim Flory

Roho Publishing
4040 Graphic Arts Road Emporia, KS 66801
www.rohopublishing.com

About Roho Publishing

When Kip Keino defeated Jim Ryun in the 1968 Olympic Games at 1500 meters he credited the win to "Roho." Roho is the Swahili word for spirit demonstrated through extraordinary strength and courage. The type of courage and strength that can be summoned up from deep within that will allow you to meet your goals and overcome the challenges in life. Roho Publishing focuses on the spirit of life and is designed to inspire, encourage, motivate and teach valuable life lessons.

Dedication

To all coaches who work with young people on a daily basis and make a difference. You make a difference in developing not only the physical components, but also the hearts and minds of athletes.

Acknowledgements

We would like to thank all the coaches we have had over the years who made a difference in our lives. We would also like to thank the athletes whom we have had the privilege to coach over the years. Each of these individuals have taught us so much about the qualities to be successful in life—good character, integrity, a strong work ethic, dedication, and perseverance.

Index

Introduction

The most important thing in the Olympic Games is not to win but to take part, just as the most important thing in life is not the triumph but the struggle. The essential thing is not to have conquered but to have fought well. – The Olympic Creed

"Motivational Moments in 2016 Olympic Track and Field" is designed to inspire, encourage, motivate, and teach us valuable life lessons. The stories are written for those who are currently competing, coaching, have participated in track and field, or are simply a track and field or sports fan. The questions at the end of the stories are designed to challenge, teach, and enable you to grow as you apply these principles to athletics and to the bigger game of life.

All of the athletes are ordinary people who used extraordinary desire to accomplish extraordinary things. Each athlete began simply with a dream, which developed into a belief in themselves. They personify the Olympic philosophy – *"there are no great people, rather there are great challenges that ordinary people are forced to meet."* Their stories offer hope that we can dream and reach beyond our perceived abilities and achieve personal satisfaction.

The stories are rich in history and designed to be read in a few minutes. The stories pay honor to all the young men and women who enter the arena, who make the attempt, and pursue excellence. These stories of great athletes teach us how to eliminate negative thinking, to focus our attention on what is important, and how to overcome obstacles to reach our goals.

Athletes throughout the past century have entered the competitive arena and competed with honor. Although not all athletes are fortunate to catch an Olympic star, all athletes can valiantly reach for the heavens. Their stories of inspiration should be read and remembered. For it has been written, *"The honor should not alone go to those who have not fallen; rather all honor to those who fall and rise again."*

This book was designed to be enjoyed by anyone with an interest in track and field. If you are a coach, you are encouraged to use these stories to motivate and inspire your athletes. Coaching is one of the most influential professions in our society. Coaches work with young people on a daily basis and have a tremendous opportunity to make a difference.

Our young people need strong role models. The athletes profiled display the drive, motivation, and dedication to train for years to reach a goal. Their stories teach the values of self-discipline, responsibility, accountability, and loyalty. They demonstrate the qualities necessary to be successful in life—good character, integrity, a strong work ethic, dedication, and perseverance.

Devon Allen

Living the Dream

Devon Allen was living the dream competing in both track and field and football for the powerhouse University of Oregon teams. He had surprisingly won the NCAA Championships as a freshman in the 110-meter hurdles and then shocked the pros by winning the USATF Championships two weeks later on his home track in Eugene. The following football season found the Ducks making the National Championship semifinal game and Devon back to return the opening kick-off. As Devon made his way up field, he was tackled and remained on the ground. A torn anterior cruciate ligament not only ended his season but cast doubt on his future as a track and field athlete.

It was during this time that Devon turned to and found time to practice religion. Although he grew up in a religious family, he was never baptized as a child. The time away from the football field and track gave him time to grow closer to his religion.

Although he spent the spring of 2015 rehabilitating his knee, he still found himself wishing he could be out on the track. Therefore, instead of being in the Hayward Field stands during the NCAA Track and Field Championships, he was doing service work in the Dominican Republic.

He returned in 2016 and won the NCAA Championship in the 110 hurdles. Though previously doubted by many, Devon's dream of making the 2016 Olympic team in the 110-meter hurdles was starting to become a genuine possibility.

Just two days before he was set to compete in the 110-meter hurdles finals at the Olympic Trials, Devon was baptized in the Willamette River in Eugene. His prayers were answered when Devon ran 13.03 over the 110-meter race, securing his spot on the Olympic team.

Devon debuted in his first international meet at the 2016 Olympics. He ran 13.31 but was only able to place 5th as an American failed to win a medal in the event for the first time ever. Devon Allen is a shining example of a positive role model who has overcome adversity to excel at the highest level.

Questions For Thought:

1. Devon was unable to compete due to an injury, yet came back stronger that ever. What does it take to come back once you have been down?
2. During Devon's injury he was able to focus on important things like family, relationships and religion. Think about how important those things are to you. Do you keep sports in the proper focus relative to the other important things in your life?
3. Devon finishes strong over the last few hurdles. What does it mean to you to "finish strong over barriers?"

Nia Ali

Olympic Persistence

Nia Ali has overcome many hurdles both on and off the track to become an Olympian. She began her running career at the age of six as a distance runner, in addition to playing basketball and softball. She gave the hurdles a try as a senior in high school, and went on to place in the top 10 at USA Juniors. Because of her athletic versatility, she toyed with the heptathlon, high jump, and hurdles during her first year of college at the University of Tennessee, winning the SEC heptathlon title her freshman year. As a city girl, she struggled with the slow-paced lifestyle in Knoxville, so she transferred to the University of Southern California, where she continued competing in both the hurdles and heptathlon.

Nia was faced with tragedy in 2009, when her father died in a murder-suicide back home in Philadelphia. He drove his mistress home one morning, shooting and then turning the gun on himself. Nia became so overwhelmed with grief and second-guessing in the months following the tragedy that she shut herself off from the rest of the world, crawling inside her emptiness, all alone except for her demons. Nia was determined to come back stronger than ever after sitting out the 2010 season, returning in 2011 to win the NCAA and World University titles. She credits USC assistant Dr. Tommie White with helping her overcome her grief.

In 2013, Nia was third at USA Outdoors, earning a spot to compete in Moscow for her first World Championships. However, it was Ali's coach, Ryan Wilson, who saw success in this meet by claiming second place in the 110-meter hurdles, while Nia failed to qualify for the finals. Just a few months later though, Ali shocked the world and claimed her spot among the best in the world, as she became the 2014 World Indoor 60 meter hurdle champion with a 7.80.

As soon as Nia thought she was on the road to the 2015 World Championships in Beijing, she learned she was pregnant. Although many track and field athletes consider this career suicide, Nia set her sights on Rio 2016 and she continued with her usual training regime for the first four months of her pregnancy. She then decided to stay fit yet relax with her family back in Philadelphia from that point on, knowing she would have to begin serious training once she returned to Los Angeles after the birth of her son.

Just 15 months later, her son, Titus Maximus, took a victory lap with his mom after she won a silver medal in the 100-meter hurdles at the Rio Olympic Games. For the first time in history, the US women completed a 1-2-3 sweep in the event.

Questions For Thought:

1. Nia Ali faced multiple setbacks to become an Olympic medalist. How can setbacks make you stronger?
2. Do you have a plan B if plan A does not work out?
3. Nia benefits from the challenges of tough competition in the U.S. women's hurdles. How can good competition within your team help you?

Almaz Ayana

Smashing the World Record

Ethiopia's Almaz Ayana set a blistering pace in the final of the women's 2016 Olympic 10,000-meter race and no one thought she could keep it. But she did. Not only did she break the 23-year-old world record, she obliterated it by 14 seconds, running 29:17.45.

Almaz pulled away from the field midway through the race and ran the second half in 14:30.64, meaning her 5000 meter split was more than 10 seconds faster than the 5K Olympic record. She bested second place, Kenya's Vivian Cheruiyot, by almost 15 seconds.

That race may be considered the greatest 10,000-meter in history, as it yielded eight national records—Ethiopia, Kenya, United States, Sweden, Burundi, Greece, Kyrgyzstan, and Uzbekistan—and 18 personal bests.

However, at a time when distance running was tainted with doping scandals, skepticism arose about Almaz's legitimacy. When asked about the allegations, Almaz smiled and said, "My doping is my training. My doping is Jesus."

The race in Rio was just the second time she had competed at the 10,000-meter distance. Almaz spent her early track and field years believing she was a steeplechaser. That was largely her focus up until 2013, when she began to concentrate more on the flat events. She debuted at the 10,000 distance a month and a half before taking the Olympic gold. She ran her first attempt in 30:07 and defeated compatriot Tirunesh Dibaba, one of the most decorated distance runners in history.

It's not a coincidence that Almaz defeated Dibaba for the first time in a 10,000-meter race, as they both hail from the same area of Bekoji, a rural mountain community of about 16,000. The town alone has produced an extraordinary number of Olympians, its runners winning 10 gold Olympic medals in track and field.

Almaz had her eyes set on the 5000 meter gold as well, and entered as the favorite. She looked to be on the way to another victory when she surged into a large lead four laps into the race, but was unable to hold off Kenya's Vivian Cheruiyot and Hellen Onsando Obiri. She finished in third.

Questions For Thought:

1. Almaz is a very aggressive runner. How aggressive are you in your quest to achieve your goal?
2. How important is the environment that you are in? What factors in your environment can make you better?
3. The women's 10K final produced numerous records. How do you respond when the level of competition is high?

Mutaz Barshim

National Pioneer

Mutaz Barshim of Qatar used to skip practice and show up late when his new coach, Stanislaw Szczyrba (Stanley), took over. Stanley would make the high jumper run 1500s and Mutaz's poor attitude and effort made Stanley want to leave Qatar after just four months of coaching.

Though the duo didn't click right away, Stanley kept a watchful eye on Mutaz and told him he could be jumping 7-6 by the end of the year. For someone who was only currently jumping 7-0, it was hard to believe. Stanley asked Mutaz to quit school at Qatar University and use his natural talent to dedicate himself solely to the high jump. Within one year, he was clearing 7-6 to become the 2010 world junior champion. He and Stanley had earned each others' trust. Together, they share a sense of humor but also share success. They've won Olympic bronze in London 2012, silver at the 2013 Worlds in Moscow, and gold at the 2014 World Indoor Championships before pulling off the second-highest jump in history at the 2014 Diamond League series in Brussels—a 7-11 ½ jump that placed him just ¾ of an inch short of the world record, set in 1993.

But in the Olympic year, it wasn't about clearing heights or breaking the world record. The focus was on building endurance in order to persevere through qualification jumps at the Olympics. He took off many Diamond League meets in order to focus on bringing home another Olympic medal for Qatar.

Mutaz entered the 2016 Olympic competition as the world leader. However, he was bested by the man who shared bronze with him in London – Canada's Derek Drouin. His second place finish was the best result by a Qatar citizen in any sport in the history of the Olympics. With a bronze in London and silver in Rio, Mutaz looks ahead to win gold at the 2020 Olympics, but can't forget about what's in between.

Questions For Thought:

1. Mutaz Barshim improved his work habits and improved his jumping. In what areas could your work habits improve?
2. Mutaz's coach challenged him. Who challenges you?
3. How do you respond to the challenge?

Tianna Bartoletta

New Year: No Limit

At the young age of 19, Tianna Madison was a world champion in the long jump. But early success did not translate to consistent success at the world-class level. She fell out of world-class shape and dealt with financial difficulties, including bankruptcy and a foreclosure. She continued competing to earn money to pay for school tuition, but was embarrassed by her performances. She thought it was her time to move on.

In 2012, she married investment manager John Bartoletta, who played a key role in helping her get back on her feet financially and supported her new journey back to the track scene. On New Year's eve of 2012, she made the decision to re-commit to the sport of track and field. Her motto became "New Year: No Limit." Tianna commuted three hours one way daily to train with her coach, Rana Reider, for 220 consecutive days and she improved her diet, focusing on carbohydrates, protein, vegetables, and water.

This change in training and diet led Tianna to a spot on the 2012 Olympic team. In London, she earned a gold medal as part of the 4x100 meter relay team and a fourth place finish in the 100 meter finals, just .04 from a medal.

After her 2012 Summer Olympic performance, Tianna was named to the U.S. Bobsled team, where she competed alongside fellow track and field Olympians Lolo Jones and Hyleas Fountain. Tianna and her teammate finished third in her first World Cup bobsledding competition.

She is launching Club 360, a primarily online outreach program for young girls. She said she came up with the idea several years ago, while still struggling herself.

Tianna made the Olympic team in the long jump and 100-meter. Although she failed to make the 100 final, she ran on the U.S. 4x100 team that took Olympic gold. Tianna delivered on her second to last jump in the long jump, jumping a personal best of 23-6 ¼ to win the Olympic long jump over American teammate Brittney Reeese. New Year, No Limits.

Questions For Thought:

1. Tianna found success early and then lost her focus. What are some ways you use to help you re-focus?
2. Tianna made a commitment to pay the price in training. What price are you willing to pay to become better?
3. The slogan Tianna used was "New Year: No Limit." What limitations do you place on yourself? How could you remove those limitations?

Boris Berian

Fast Track to Success

In 2015, Boris Berian would wake up early and walk or ride his bike three miles each way to his job at McDonalds in Colorado Springs. In 2016, Boris Berian was lining up on the track in Rio De Janeiro against the fastest 800-meter runners in the world.

In 2012, Boris had won two NCAA Division II 800-meter titles while at Adams State University. After realizing school was not for him and dropping out in the spring of 2014, Boris was sleeping on a friend's couch while working the McDonald's day shift. He trained on a dirt track at night, using and adapting workouts from a training log he used at Adams State.

When he received a message from a member of the Big Bear Track Club inviting him to train with the club, Boris saw it as perfect timing. The only requirements were to work hard and to have a positive attitude. The Big Bear Track Club is an elite training club based in Big Bear Lake, California, formed by 800-meter world medalist Brenda Martinez and her coach/husband, Carlos Handler.

Boris shocked the world and emerged onto the international scene by winning the 2016 IAAF World Indoor championship in the 800. He ran the opening 200 in 23.92, a strategy that even Boris himself called "crazy." In just nine months of training with the Big Bear Track Club, Boris lowered his time from 1:48.89 to 1:43.34. Months before the 2016 Olympic Trials, Boris was faced with a challenge of fighting an endorsement lawsuit with Nike.

Through confidence and resiliency, Boris incidentally became an advocate for athletes' rights. At the Trials, he did not get to the front early and was caught late by Clayton Murphy. Still, Boris finished second in 1:44.92 and made his first Olympic Team. His improbable Olympic odyssey came to an end when he finished 8th in the 800 meter Olympic final. He was in contact with the leaders until the 600-meter mark but began to tie up with 200 meters to go. Boris Berian's meteoric rise from fast food worker to Olympian may seem like a fairy tale story. There has been, however, many barriers that he has overcome with a positive attitude and a hard work ethic.

Questions For Thought:

1. Boris likes to go out fast and control the race. How do you take control of things?
2. Boris paid his dues. What dues have you paid on the way to success?
3. What dues are you willing to pay?

Gwen Berry

The American Record Holder that Wasn't

The day before the 2016 Olympic Trials, hammer thrower Gwen Berry was on suspension. The next day, she made the Olympic team.

In June, the United States Anti-Doping Agency (USADA) announced that Gwen had used a prohibited medication and was given a three-month sanction for her rule violation. Gwen declared the use of an inhaler containing Vilanterol Trifenatate, a prohibited substance, during an in-competition sample collection at the USATF Indoor Track and Field Championships. Gwen was using the prescribed medication to treat asthma under the care of a physician rather than as an effort to enhance her performance. Though the results of that in-competition test were negative, her three-month ineligibility began March 29, the date the USADA received the results of the test.

In addition, Gwen was disqualified from all results obtained on or after March 11, 2016. This includes her American Record hammer throw of 250-4 at the Tuscan Elite Classic in May. Within three months she had broken the American Record and lost it, finished first in the IAAF Hammer Throw Challenge and lost it, and missed out on $30,000 in bonuses from sponsors. She was publicly shamed and her reputation was tainted.

The day after her suspension ended, she finished second behind Amber Campbell with a throw of 239-2 to earn one of the three tickets on the U.S. team to Rio. Though she could only manage a 229-3 throw in the qualifying rounds in Rio and did not advance to the final, Gwen Berry has displayed a never-give up attitude.

Questions For Thought:

1. Although Gwen did not purposely cheat, athletes are responsible for knowing the rules and what they ingest. Are you careful with what you put in your body?
2. Gwen lost money and her reputation was damaged. If your reputation suffers, what can you do to repair it?
3. Do you have any medical conditions such as asthma? How can one still compete at a high level and manage a medical condition?

Ben Blankenship

Making the Team

Ben Blankenship and Leo Manzano are no strangers in the 1500 meter event. Just .02 seconds separated Blankenship from Manzano at the 2015 U.S. Championships, giving Manzano a berth at the World Championships while Blankenship stayed home. Which is why Blankenship wanted a do-over at the 2016 U.S. Trials. He had that incentive to rally down the homestretch the same way he did a year earlier, this time to beat Manzano and clench his spot in Rio.

During the 2012 Olympic year, Ben was out with a hip injury during his final season at the University of Minnesota. Though he was working for a friend's excavation business, he knew he would eventually return to the sport. An invitation to join the Oregon Track Club Elite in 2013 reset his career, and since then he has established himself as one of the top 1500-meter runners in the country.

Ben burst onto the national scene in 2015, taking silver in both the one mile and two mile at the U.S. Indoor Track and Field Championships, placing fourth in the 1500 meters at the U.S. Outdoor Track and Field Championships and anchoring the Team USA Distance Medley Relay to a world record at the World Relays. The season did include some disappointment, with the fourth place finish at the U.S. outdoor championships—missing the world championships team by .02 of a second.

In Rio, Ben finished ninth among 15 runners in the fast heat to qualify for the semifinals. He then went on to finish fourth in his semifinal heat, running more than a second slower that his qualifying heat, but yet qualifying for the final. He made some tactical mistakes in a slow-paced final, running on the outside of the 12-man field in third place before moving to the inside and settling in fifth. He briefly took the lead from American Matthew Centrowitz at the half-mile mark before falling back in the final 400 meters to finish in eighth at 3:51.09.

Questions For Thought:

1. Ben wanted a "do-over." Are there any "do-overs" you would like to have?
2. In close races decided by mere hundredths of a second, what factors decide the race?
3. Would having mental skills be an advantage if competitors have similar physical skills?

Usain Bolt

Lightning Bolt

From his first gold medal in the 100 meters at the 2008 Olympics in Beijing, Jamaica's Usain Bolt started a streak—or rather, a bolt of what would become a career of victory. Since becoming an otherworldly figure in 2008, Usain has won 69 of 74 races. He won 18 of 19 championship races in the 100 meters, 200 meters and 4x100-meter relay, and his only "loss" was in the 2011 world championships, when he was disqualified for a false start.

Usain, the world record holder in the 100 at 9.58 seconds and the 200 at 19.19 seconds, had raced little in the 2016 season. He was running strong in June of 2016, and clocked 9.87 at a meet in Kingston, Jamaica, despite stumbling twice. But three weeks later at the Jamaican Olympic Trials, Usain strained his low back and left hamstring, which have often given him problems in the past. He qualified for Rio due to the medical exemptions that the Jamaican team allows in the qualifying process despite not competing in the trials.

In Rio, he took the gold medal in the 100 meters for the third consecutive time; a feat accomplished only twice by Carl Lewis. Usain easily ran down fast-starting Justin Gatlin of the U.S. and crossed the line in 9.81 seconds, his fastest time in a year that's been sabotaged by injuries. At age 29, it was the slowest of his three Olympic 100-meter finals. In the 200, he believed he could break his world record of 19.19 and could even go under 19 seconds in the final, but he crossed the line in 19.78 seconds, his slowest time in his three Olympic 200 meter finals. Usain finished out his Olympic career in style. In the 4x100 relay, Jamaica took home gold, beating out Japan and a United States team that was later disqualified due to a lane violation. With his third gold medal of these Olympic Games, Usain was able to get the legendary triple-triple, making him the greatest sprinter of all time.

Usain Bolt plans to retire next year after the world track and field championships in London, with one transcendent career goal remaining: to take his world record of 19.19 seconds at 200 meters below the 19-second barrier.

Questions For Thought:

1. Usain has performed at a consistently high level. What is the key to a consistent performance?
2. What traits does Usain possess that has made him so successful?
3. Usain stays relaxed and keeps his poise. What techniques do you use to stay relaxed?

Tori Bowie

Fighting Back

Tori Bowie was an outstanding basketball player at Pisgah High School in Sand Hill, Mississippi. The talent seemed to run in her family. In fact, her and her cousins made up the starting five of their school's basketball team. There was no track team, but when a new head basketball coach saw the girls excelling on the court, she turned that basketball team into the first girl's track team. Despite the lack of a track to train on, the team won state in its first year of existence and repeated it the following year. Tori contributed to the team effort by setting long jump records. She continued her track career at the University of Southern Mississippi, where she won two national championships and was a six-time All-American.

Things didn't always come easy and the path wasn't always clear for Tori. She grew up in foster care until she was taken in and raised by her grandmother.

After the second of her two NCAA titles, she qualified for the 2012 Olympic Trials in the long jump, but suffered a broken jaw while celebrating her performance at a club in Mississippi. She was an innocent bystander who got hit in the jaw with a bottle as a fight broke out. The injury ended her season and Tori watched the Trials and the Olympics from home. Tori set the stage for Rio by winning a gold medal in the 100 meters in the 2015 IAAF Championships. She made the Olympic team in both the 100 and 200 meters by placing 3rd in the 100 and 1st in the 200. The Rio Olympic Games would be Tori's greatest stage. Tori earned a silver medal in the 100, running 10.8 despite having a slow start out of the blocks. Tori improved her start in the 200 final and was running fifth coming off the curve, but fought her way to a bronze medal in 22.15.

Tori's Olympic Games would include a third medal to complete the set of gold, silver, and bronze. The U.S. took the gold after having to qualify for the final by posting a fast time in the semi, running by themselves due to being fouled in the prelims. Bowie anchored the team in 41.01, the second best time ever, despite having to run the tight curves of lane one.

Tori's original goal was to become a dentist. However, her track and field skills led her in a different direction to a professional track and field career. The former long jumper is now one of the fastest women in the world. Tori Bowie is an inspiration to youth to believe even though they are from a small school they can go do great things.

Questions For Thought:

1. Tori's high school team won the state track and field championship despite not having a track to train on. Do you accept things as they are, or adapt to succeed?
2. Tori inspires youth by being a great role model. Who is your role model?
3. What qualities do you have that may be a role model to others?

Thiago Braz da Silva

Home Country Hero

The Rio Olympic Games pole vault competition was more like a marathon, lasting until after midnight. Because of strong winds and a torrential rain storm the competition was delayed for an hour after just a few vaults. When the competition started again, it was still raining. Many fans had left the stadium as the competition on the track had ended over an hour earlier. France's Renaud Lavillenie was the overwhelming favorite as the holder of the world's highest pole vault ever. Lavellenie was trying to become only the second man in history to win two Olympic titles.

As the competition continued down to only six men left, Lavellenie was in the driver's seat, having cleared all three of his vaults. The pressure was on his competitors as they all needed to equal or beat their personal best to beat him. All of Lavellenie's competitors failed except one, the hometown hero from Brazil, Thiago Braz da Silva. Thiago cleared on his second attempt and the competition was down to a two-man battle with Lavellenie and Braz da Silva. Lavellenie had not missed all night and he soared over his first attempt at an Olympic record of 19-7 ½ as the rains fell again and caused a 20-minute delay.

Lavellenie had cleared that height many times in his outstanding career. Thiago had never cleared the height, yet what he did next was extraordinary. He passed on the Olympic record height, and the bar was raised to a height far higher than he had ever achieved before, 19-9 ¼.

Amazingly, he made it on his second attempt to achieve his personal best performance. Meanwhile, the pressure had shifted to Lavellenie, who had failed on his first two attempts. The crowd who had been wildly cheering their countryman Thiago, started to boo as Lavellenie took the runway for his final attempt as he brushed the bar with his knee.

Thiago Braz da Silva, the kid from Sao Paolo competing in his very first Olympics, who had never even won a Diamond League meeting, much less a medal at the World Championships became Brazil's new national hero. He became the first Brazilian man to get an Olympic gold medal in 32 years.

Questions For Thought:

1. Thiago became a national hero. Who are your heroes?
2. How do you use the home field to your advantage?
3. Despite being the underdog, Thiago passed on a height he had never cleared before in a tremendous display of confidence. How do you develop your confidence?

Donavan Brazier

Freshman Sensation

As a freshman at Texas A&M, middle distance runner Donavan Brazier made history at the 2016 NCAA Championships. Brazier set a new American junior record and broke the NCAA 800-meter record in 1:43.55 on the 50th anniversary of Jim Ryun's previous record of 1:44.3. This put him at number eight all-time on the U.S. 800 list with the third-fastest time in the world in 2016. He then decided to forgo the rest of his NCAA eligibility to turn professional, signing a contract with Nike.

Donavan had originally decided to run at World Juniors, but entered the Olympic Trials just two weeks after his record setting performance. The men's 800 was surprising to say the least, as two 2012 Olympians and one collegiate record holder wouldn't make the U.S. team.

Donavan led the field through 700 meters in a qualifying round; however, he locked up on the homestretch, which resulted in a fourth-place finish out of heat four. He finished in 1:48.13, less than a second behind the top three and did not advance to the next round. Donavan's agent protested, arguing another runner stepped on his shoe in the first 200 meters, which affected him in the final stages in the race, but USATF denied the protest. Donavan's Olympic dream was put on hold.

After the Trials, Donavan moved from College Station, Texas to Florida to train with Duane Solomon his coach, Johnny Gray. Gray, who is a four-time Olympian and Olympic bronze medalist, as well as the American record holder, has coached Solomon to a fourth place finish at the 2012 Olympics and sixth at the 2013 world championships. The duo is 1-2 on the American all-time list.

Despite failing to make the Olympic team, Donavan Brazier's outstanding freshman season has set the stage for a bright future.

Questions For Thought:

1. Jim Ryun's 800-meter collegiate record lasted for 50 years. Who are your heroes that competed many years ago?
2. What can you learn from those legendary athletes?
3. Experience can be a valuable tool. Think about how you can use your past experiences to create better performances.

Trayvon Bromell

Mindset of Spirit

Trayvon Bromell was on a streak. Unfortunately, it was a bad-luck injury streak. In three consecutive years he severely injured his left knee on a back flip while in the eighth grade. The next year he damaged a right knee while rebounding, and followed that up as a high school sophomore with a fractured hip in a 100-meter race. After three trips to the hospital, Trayvon was ready to give it up. Fortunately, he didn't.

The inspiration to go to the Olympics was first planted in his head while playing the video game "Athens 2004" before one of his track meets. He had never considered or even watched the Olympics, but from then on out, he strove to become a character in that game. He was named Gatorade's national track and field athlete of the year in 2013. He ran the fastest time ever (9.99 seconds) by a U.S. prep athlete, and he also won the USA Junior Championships.

After two NCAA titles at Baylor, he turned pro. He tied for the bronze medal in the 100 meter at the 2015 World Championships in Beijing and won a World Indoor Championship in the 60 meter in 2016. Despite turning pro and foregoing his NCAA eligibility, Trayvon plans to return to Baylor to finish his degree. He also wants to start a foundation to help others fulfill their dreams in his Florida community.

Trayvon's stature, just 5-9 and 156 pounds, stands out, especially among Usain Bolt's 6-5, 205-pound build. He doesn't let that stop him or let others' instill fear in him.

He told the Tampa Bay Times, "It all comes down to who has strongest mindset. A lot of people don't see me as a big threat, because of my stature and size. A lot of people count me out, just because people are bigger than me. At the end of the day, if you have a stronger mindset you can overpower anyone."

Trayvon qualified for the finals in the 100-meter dash in Rio, but could only manage a 10.08 for 8th place among sliver medalist Justin Gatlin and Bolt. With his strong mindset, look for Trayvon Bromell to compete for several years for the "fastest man in the world" title.

Questions For Thought:

1. Despite numerous injuries at a young age, Trayvon never gave up. What keeps you from giving up?
2. Trayvon doesn't use his body size as an excuse. How many excuses do you use? Could you turn that excuse into something positive and productive?
3. Trayvon has a strong mindset that has led him to success. On a scale of 1-10 what is the strength of your mindset?

Michelle Carter

Shot Put Diva

Michelle Carter didn't even know her father, Michael Carter, had won an Olympic medal and a Super Bowl ring in the same year. That is, until a junior high teacher encouraged her to try the shot put.

Her father ensured the shot put had been her choice and had been careful not to put any pressure on Michelle to follow in his footsteps, as he had won silver in the shot put in the 1984 Olympics. But as it turns out, she did.

Her career began by earning a silver medal at the 2001 World Youth Championships, the first time she had gone out of the country to throw. Since then, she has become a force to reckon with on the international scene. She competed in the 2008 Beijing Olympics, where she finished just 15th. Since 2012, though, she has finished in the top five at all six major global championships indoor and outdoor and finished 5th at the London Olympics.

But after the 2012 Olympics, she became tired, frustrated, and developed low self-esteem when her off-season weight gain didn't come off when she returned to her training regimen and was ultimately diagnosed with hypothyroidism.

Although ninety pounds heaver, Michelle didn't allow her condition to effect the person she was inside. She is a proponent of positive body image and runs a positive sports confidence camp for young female throwers. Considering herself to be a girly-girl, Michelle, a certified professional make-up artist, has been deemed the "Shot Put Diva." She also posed for ESPN's body issue and tries to encourage and send young women the message that muscles are cool.

These are the very same muscles that helped propel Michelle to an American Record in 2013, throwing 66-4 ¾, a throw that would send her confidence into a whirlwind, gaining momentum with each competition. In Rio, it appeared New Zealand's Valerie Adams would win her third consecutive gold medal in the event when Carter stepped into the ring for her final throw. She had come from behind to win her last two major championships, the 2016 World Indoors (where she set an American Indoor record) and the Olympic Trials on her final throw. Michelle Carter catapulted the shot 67-8 ¼, breaking the American Record and becoming the first American woman to capture gold in the event.

Questions For Thought:

1. Michelle's father was an Olympic silver medalist, but did not push Michelle into the sport. How do you handle expectations?
2. Michelle has struggled with thyroid problems but is a role model encouraging others on self-esteem. Is your self-esteem separate from your athletic performance?
3. Michelle has learned to adapt and thrive in big moments. How can your routine develop the confidence for you to perform when it counts?

Kristi Castlin

Completing the Sweep

Kristi Castlin's road to Rio was a long and winding journey and she had a mission to complete it. When she was 12, her father was murdered during a botched robbery inside the motel he worked nights at. His killer wasn't sent to prison until nearly 15 years later, in April of 2016, but it was the motivation Kristi needed to put the tragedy behind her and move forward with her dreams. Through the challenging years, Kristi grew into one of the fastest women in the world in one of the most competitive events in United States track and field, the 100-meter hurdles.

Running came easy to Kristi, as both of her parents were athletic. Kristi was already involved in cheerleading and gymnastics, and her mom, a single mother to two active children, wanted to keep her children focused on academics and didn't think she could handle adding track to the schedule. But when she saw Kristi hurdle for the first time, she knew it was for her.

Kristi was the state champion three years in a row in the 100-meter hurdles and won state her senior year in the 300-meter hurdles. Although she competed in relays, she preferred the hurdles as it was a way to be different. She went on to compete at Virginia Tech, where she earned the honor of ACC Freshman of the Year in 2007. But before her freshman year was over, Kristi once again experienced a gun violence tragedy when a student at Virginia Tech shot and killed 32 people and wounded 17 others before committing suicide. The mass shooting at her school reminded her of the pain her and her family endured after her father was killed.

Kristi finished in second place in the 100-meter hurdles at the Olympic trials in Eugene, Oregon, earning her a spot on the United States team headed to the Rio games. She dedicated her second place finish to survivors of gun violence.

In the 100-meter hurdle final, Kristi was near the back but her confidence in her ability to close allowed her to rally into third. The U.S. threesome of Brianna Rollins, Nia Ali, and Kristi Castlin went 1-2-3 at Rio in the 100-meter hurdles. It was the first 100-meter hurdle sweep in Olympic history as well as the first-ever 1-2-3 by American women in any event.

Questions For Thought:

1. Kristi overcame tragedy and used it as motivation. What setbacks have you overcome?
2. Kristi chose the challenging event of the hurdles so she could be different. How often do you take the difficult path?
3. Kristi dedicated her Olympics to gun violence survivors. What do you do outside your sport to help society?

Matthew Centrowitz

Like Father Like Son

"Like father like son." The phrase is tattooed across Matthew Centrowitz's chest and he's proud to show it off. That's because Matthew and his father, who goes by Matt, are almost one in the same. For starters, they share a name, but they also attended the University of Oregon, ran the 1500 meters, and are both two-time Olympians.

After missing a medal by .04 seconds in 2012, Matthew was determined to let it fuel him, not frighten him. Between winning the 1500 at the 2016 Indoor World Championships and the last three U.S. Championships he competed in (2013, 2015, and 2016 indoors), and being the most confident, fit, and competitive version of himself so far had him going from a first-timer in 2012 to being among the favorites in 2016.

A stress reaction in the spring of 2016 deterred his training but he was back to health with six weeks remaining before the Trials, where he closed in 53 seconds to break a 36-year-old meet record in 3:34.09 and erase any doubts about his fitness.

Matthew went from running a record-breaking time in Eugene to a race in Rio that lacked speed but made up for it with strategy. The Olympic 1500 final tends to be a slow, tactical race, and Matthew was prepared for anything fast or slow. His time, 3:50.00, was the slowest by an Olympic champion since Luigi Beccali of Italy won in 3:51.2 at the 1932 Games in Los Angeles.

Matthew led almost from start to finish, something he usually doesn't do. Ayanleh Souleiman of Djibouti, the 2014 world indoor champion at the 1500, pulled ahead of Matthew with about 500 meters remaining and ran toward the outside of lane 1. In what has become somewhat of Matthew's signature move —he had slithered through an opening along the rail at the world track and field championships twice before—he made a move along the inside rail with about 450 meters remaining and ran a blistering final lap in 50.62 seconds. His preparation and confidence gave him the ability to race well at any pace.

Matthew Centrowitz's 1500 win was an American first since Mel Sheppard took the Olympic gold medal 108 years ago.

Questions For Thought:

1. Matthew believes in his finishing kick. Do you finish well? How could you improve this?
2. Matthew runs with a very relaxed technique. How is technique developed?
3. Matthew was prepared for any possibility. How important is preparation?

Paul Chelimo

From Joy to Disappointment to Joy

Paul Chelimo thought he had won the silver medal in the 5000 meters in the 2016 Olympic Games. Then three athletes were disqualified for stepping on or inside the line on the inside of the track. When Paul was being interviewed for his second place finish, he was informed on live television he had been disqualified. A shocked and disappointed Paul had just heard his silver medal was gone and wanted to appeal. After the U.S. appealed the decision, it was ruled that Paul had taken one step out but it had no impact on the race. The appeal was successful and Paul had his medal back, picking up the first medal for the U.S. in the event since 1964.

Paul grew up in Kenya and ran first at Shorter University in Georgia and then at the University of North Carolina, Greensboro. Runners from Kenya often run in universities in the U.S. but return home when they are done with college. However, the military has a World Class Athlete Program that allows those who qualify to basically train full time while serving in the U.S. Military. By joining the military, foreign athletes can get expedited U.S. citizenship. Normally, naturalization can take up to five years, but those serving in the U.S. military can become citizens after they complete basic training. Paul joined the Army in 2014 and became a citizen in time to run for the U.S. at the 2016 Olympics. Eleven members of the Army's World Class Athlete Program went to Rio, and Paul was one of four Kenyan-born runners in the contingent.

Sixteen runners made the Olympic 5000-meter final, including Paul, who had the slowest personal best time of all the runners competing. Paul caught a break when the pace slowed early in the race and he ran among the top three runners. With a fast and furious finish in the final lap, Paul almost fell twice when his feet became entangled other runners, but he maintained his balance and gave chase to Mo Farah, coming within six-tenths of a second from winning.

Paul Chelimo's achievement was remarkable. He had barely made the U.S. team in the Olympic Trials, but peaked to run a PR of 13.19.54 in the semis, and then ran another PR, improving by 15 seconds to 13:03.90 to win a silver medal at the Olympics.

Questions For Thought:

1. Paul rose to the level of the competition, running far faster than he ever had before. How do you rise to the level of competition?
2. Paul represents the U.S. with pride. Do you represent with pride?
3. What factors all came together to allow Paul to perform his remarkable achievement?

Will Claye

Best Day Ever

Will Claye was born in Arizona shortly after his parents migrated from Sierra Leone in West Africa to the United States. Had his parents not left, he could have been born near the start of Sierra Leone's 12-year civil war, a war in which boys his age were forced to be child soldiers. He could have led a much different life than that of a two-time Olympian.

In 2012, Will became the only Olympian to medal in both the long jump and the triple jump in the past 80 years, winning a bronze and silver at the London Olympics. He was envisioning a different color of medal in Rio, but only got one chance to do so. Although he finished in the top three in the long jump at the 2016 Olympic Trials, Will was just one centimeter short of reaching the Olympic qualifying mark of 26-9. He had been bothered by back and toe injuries throughout the early part of 2016 and 2015.

After missing out on a spot on the 2016 Olympic team once already in the long jump, Will won the Olympic Trials triple jump with a distance of 57-11, the third-best jump of his career, over friend, rival and fellow Florida Gator Christian Taylor.

Four years prior, Taylor and Will went 1-2 at the London Olympics. In Rio, they repeated the performance. Will said it was the best day of his life, not only because of the Olympic silver medal, but he proposed to longtime girlfriend and Olympic hurdler, Queen Harrison. Though Will's focus was on the competition when it mattered, he couldn't keep up with Taylor, who jumped 58-7 ¼ on his first attempt and Will jumped 58-3 ¼.

Questions For Thought:

1. Will was fortunate to grow up in better circumstances than he could have had his parents not moved to the United States. How much control do you have over your circumstances?
2. Will and Christian Taylor have had a friendly rivalry since becoming teammates at the University of Florida. Do you have any friendly competitions with any of your teammates?
3. Will had big plans to propose to his girlfriend after competition, but managed to stay focused. How do you stay focused when your mind is on other things?

Kerron Clement

He Runs the World

As the Beyoncé song asks, "Who run the world? Girls!" the answer should in fact, actually be Kerron Clement. Kerron was chosen to appear as an actor in Beyoncé's music video for her hit song back in 2011 before he was known as a two-time world champion, three-time Olympian, and two-time Olympic gold medalist.

After winning a 4x400 meter gold medal and a 400-meter hurdles silver medal at the 2008 Beijing Olympics, Kerron, a native of Trinidad and Tobago who went to high school in Texas, set out to re-establish himself him among the favorites at the 400 hurdles in Rio.

At the 2012 London Olympics, Kerron finished last in the 400-meter hurdles final and had dealt with injuries and surgeries, from his groin to a hernia. He took a break from competition in 2014 to allow his mind and body to rest. When he returned in 2015, he had discovered a newfound love for the hurdles. He finished in fourth place at the 2015 World Championships, just one-hundredth of a second from third. He was confident going into the Olympic year and even cleared out a spot in a cabinet at home, labeling it "Gold Medal 2016."

Kerron entered Rio with more confidence and momentum than ever. Kerron ran the fastest semifinal time of all the qualifying competitors for the final and the second-fastest time of the year of 48.26. In the final, it was his confidence that helped fill his trophy cabinet back home. One of Kerron's leading rivals, Puerto Rico's Javier Culson, was disqualified for a false start in the final. Then, Kerron had to hold off Kenya's Boniface Tumuti, who was just .05 behind. He ran the rest of the world into the ground, winning with a season-best time of 47.73. With his win, the United States had won seven of the past nine Olympic 400-meter hurdle titles.

Questions For Thought:

1. Kerron took a break during the 2014 season to rest his mind and body. How important is it to take time to rest and recover?
2. Kerron was so confident heading into the Olympics that he had a trophy cabinet cleared out at home for his gold medal. When you have big dreams, how confident are you that you will achieve them?
3. Members of the U.S. team have won seven of the past nine Olympic 400-meter hurdle titles. Have you ever been a part of continuing a tradition?

Emma Coburn

Successful Routine

Emma Coburn grew up in a small town in Colorado. Before Emma starred at the University of Colorado, she began running the steeplechase as a youth athlete. The steeplechase requires runners to cover seven and a half laps with hurdle barriers and seven water jumps. Emma's steeple career began at the Great Southwestern Classic. She was originally scheduled to run the only 800-meter distance at the 2007 meet, but her dad encouraged her to find another event to add in order to make the trek from Colorado to New Mexico worth the drive. Since the 2000-meter steeplechase event was open, Emma's steeple career began.

After a brilliant career at the University of Colorado in which she won three NCAA titles and was a six-time All-American, Emma turned pro and made the U.S. Olympic team in 2012, finishing 9th in the Olympic Games. Staying focused on her training, Emma set the American record in the 3000-meter steeplechase running 9:10.76 at the Prefontaine Classic in May of 2016.

Emma continues to train hard while staying relaxed, happy and confident and the recipe has worked for success. She likes to stick to a routine before her races, making sure everything goes just right and if it does not, nothing or no one else is to blame but herself. Which is why the night before her Olympic final, she left the apartment she was sharing with teammate Jenny Simpson to stay in a hotel due to a less-than-satisfying air temperature. A rigid routine follower, Emma tries to avoid superstition at all costs. She wants to ensure it is her hard work and dedication that makes her successful, not because of luck or superstition.

In just the third Olympics in which the women's steeplechase was contested, Emma and her two U.S. teammates qualified easily for the final. The race began slowly, and Emma was not hesitant to take the lead early. When Kenyan Ruth Jebet surged to the lead shortly after that, Emma remained cool and worked her way up from fourth place. She knew she had to steadily increase her pace if she wanted to get on the podium. Throughout the last lap, Emma battled for second, but Kenyan Hyvin Jepkemoi cleared the water jump slightly ahead of Emma and held her off for the silver. Emma Coburn crossed the line in third, clocking a 9:07.63—a time which, at the time, she didn't even realize was a new American record.

Questions For Thought:

1. Emma took on a tough event when she began running the steeplechase. What is your attitude like when faced with a tough event?
2. Emma focuses on being relaxed by visualizing the event she is familiar with and has run many times. Does it make you more relaxed and confident when you visualize past success?
3. Emma also focuses on being happy. How can you balance your sport by working hard and still be happy?

Kim Collins

Ageless Sprinter

Father Time has been on Kim Collins' side. He has defied studies that show sprinters peak in their mid-to-late 20s. At 40 years old, the Saint Kitts and Nevis sprinter has competed in five Olympic Games, beginning with the 1996 Games in Atlanta, when his Caribbean island made its first Summer Olympic appearance. He has won five World Championship medals, including gold in the 100 in 2003. But he never quite got that Olympic medal.

In 2012, Kim had the honor of being his country's flag bearer, and thought at the time it might be his last Olympic shot at age 36. However, when Kim decided to stay overnight in a hotel with his wife (also his coach) and kids, his team's officials withdrew him from competition as punishment. Officials from Saint Kitts and Nevis said that Kim had breached team discipline rules by leaving the athletes' village without permission for more than one night. Kim was devastated by the treatment from officials on his own team. At the time, he vowed to never compete for his country again.

But time helped heal his wound, and in 2016, he was back at the Olympics competing as the oldest sprinter in the field. When he ran a personal best of 9.93 seconds in the 100 meters earlier in the year, he became the first 40-year-old to go under 10 seconds. In a semifinal heat with Usain Bolt and Canada's Andre De Grasse, Kim finished only sixth in 10.12 and failed to advance to the finals. Bolt later won the gold medal and De Grasse the bronze.

After the Games, Kim announced that he would soon retire. While he won't share his secret to his longevity, his motto may tell it. "You just keep going and going and definitely you're going to go until your body cannot go anymore."

Questions For Thought:

1. Kim Collins attributes his longevity to proper conditioning. How much emphasis and time do you spend on conditioning?
2. Kim has made five Olympic teams. His competitive fire still burns bright. On a scale of 1-10 how would you rate your competitive fire?
3. Kim has a personal motto. What is your motto?

Amy Cragg

Redemption

Amy Cragg wanted redemption. She had spent the past four years increasing her mileage, completing more intense workouts, alternating altitude training with sea level training, and focusing on recovery. She kicked everything up about "10 levels."

In a hot Los Angeles race at the Olympic Trials marathon, the runner who finished in the most dreaded position in the 2012 Olympic Trials marathon—4th—got her redemption in 2016.

Not only did Amy make a big move in location, change training groups and coaches, but she did it in an Olympic year. Amy parted ways with Brooks and her Providence, Rhode Island-based training group to join Nike and the Bowerman Track Club for a summer training stint in Park City, Utah. Amy and her husband moved to Portland, Oregon to collaborate with Shalane Flanagan.

The two completed almost every workout together leading up to the Trials, and it was obvious they had a strategy to work as teammates and not competitors in order to both finish in the top three. Amy and Shalane took to the front within the first five miles and separated from the other top contenders by mile 10.

In the final miles, Flanagan had begun to struggle. At times, Amy would slow her pace to talk her through it, and even grabbed a water bottle to pour over Flanagan's head, seeing she was overheating. But eventually, Amy couldn't wait around. She could see Desiree Linden approaching and knew Kara Goucher wasn't far behind. She couldn't potentially put herself in the same position she wound up in 2012.

She made her move and didn't look back, crossing the line first in 2:28.20 and claiming redemption on 2012. Linden finished in second, and Flanagan in third, crossing the line and falling into her teammate's embrace.

The U.S. squad finished an amazing 6-7-9 at the Olympics with the order of finish this time being Flanagan, Linden, and Cragg.

Questions For Thought:

1. Amy displayed ultimate teamwork and the bond that builds between training mates when she helped Shalane Flanagan at the Trials. How do you help make other people better?
2. Amy amped up her training to meet her goal. How could you "amp" up your training?
3. The U.S. placed three runners in the top 10 at the Olympic marathon. Do you feel pride when you are part of a successful group?

Ryan Crouser

A Family Tradition

Ryan Crouser entered the 2016 U.S. Olympic Track and Field Trials as a slight underdog. The previous year he was ranked eighth in the United States and among his Trials competition was a world champion and two Olympic medalists. However, family history was on his side. His uncle was a two-time Olympian in the javelin. His father missed the 1984 Olympic team by only one spot in the discus, and his cousin made the 2016 Olympic team in the javelin.

Ryan's family background helped him get started early in track and field in the fifth grade in Oregon. By his sophomore year, he had set the Oregon high school state record in the discus until his cousin Sam broke it the following year. He continued to build upon his success by winning the shot put at the IAAF World Youth Championships in Italy and taking silver in the discus. He capped off his senior year in high school by breaking the national high school indoor record in the 12-pound shot at 77-2 ¾ and then the national high school record in the discus by throwing 237-6.

The majority of Ryan's family had competed at the University of Oregon, but Ryan broke the tradition by going to the University of Texas. At Texas, Ryan struggled to stay healthy, injuring a hand his freshman year. He then suffered from infections and his weight dropped dramatically, so he was forced to redshirt the 2013 indoor season. He returned with a fury by winning the outdoor NCAA championship in the shot put and followed that up with a NCAA indoor title and a NCAA outdoor title in 2014. A recurrent thumb injury ruined his chances of winning a third consecutive NCAA outdoor title, but he returned to win another NCAA indoor title, bringing his total to four NCAA championships.

Throwing in his home state of Oregon in the Olympic Trials, Ryan stepped up to the challenge by throwing a personal best of 72-6 ½ to win the Trials and qualify for the Olympic Games. The Rio Games proved to be the performance of a lifetime for Ryan. At the top of his game, Ryan posted one of the best series of throws ever with three throws over 72-7, another two over 70 feet and not a single foul in the competition. On his fifth throw of the competition, he took the lead with a monster throw of 73-10 ¾ and broke the Olympic record with the 10th best mark of all time.

A combination of family tradition, a strong work ethic and a determination to overcome setbacks has established Ryan as one of the top throwers in the world.

Questions For Thought:

1. Tradition helped Ryan succeed. How has tradition helped you succeed?
2. The Crouser family has a strong work ethic. Rate your work ethic on a scale of 1-10.
3. Ryan peaked at the right time with a PR in the Olympic Games. What is the key to achieving your peak at the right time?

Vashti Cunningham

Young Phenom

Vashti Cunningham is a bundle of the right combinations. Her neutral facial expression, effortless strain, ballerina trance, and quarterback mobility show her journey defined by a family balance.

Randall Cunningham was an ex-NFL quarterback and punter who played for four different teams, most notably being a member of the Philadelphia Eagles and the Minnesota Vikings. Now, he is the coach and father of a world champion. But he's not alone in contributing to his daughter's success.

Vashti's mother, Felicity De Jager Cunningham, was a professional ballet dancer in New York City. She was 6-foot tall and a native of South Africa. But in South Africa, they taught a ballet that favored a shorter, more compact dancer. Felicity began to practice the Balanchine technique, a ballet that extends lines and accentuates ballerinas who have tremendous jumping ability. Balanchine ballerinas have a rare ability to contort themselves in flight to make it appear as though they're almost floating through the air during their jumps.

In March 2016, Vashti Cunningham was a high school student when she won the US indoor title and the IAAF World Indoor Championships at 6-6 ¼, a world junior record. She signed a professional contract with Nike, forgoing a college career.

Her stoic facial expression has become a small smile, wave, or cheer for the crowd after a jump. She doesn't do it for herself—it's now part of her job. Her calm demeanor shows her maturity and focus required for a professional athlete with tremendous potential. The same kind of demeanor that would allow her to make her first Olympic team at 18 years old. At the U.S. Trials, she easily cleared 6-4 on her first attempt and finished second at 6-5 ½.

In Rio, Vashti struggled at 6-4 ¼ in the Olympic prelims, finally clearing it on her third attempt. After easily clearing the opening height of 6-2 in the finals, she couldn't come close to 6-4. She finished in 13th place.

With her physical and mental abilities, Vashti Cunningham is the future of U.S. women's high jumping.

Questions For Thought:

1. Vashti was a world champion while still in high school. If you had early success in an activity, how can you sustain it?
2. What do you have potential in? How do you plan to develop that potential?
3. Vashti demonstrates great focus. How are your focus skills? What are you doing to improve them?

Abbey D'Agostino

Courageous Sportsmanship

At the 2012 Olympic Trials, Abbey D'Agostino was 0.19 seconds away from making the Olympic team in the women's 5000-meter run. In one of the slimmest margins for a long distance race in the history of the U.S. Trials, Abbey finished a disappointing fifth, missing out on the top three and a chance to represent the U.S in the Olympic Games.

Abbey had earned seven NCAA championship honors running for Dartmouth. She ran professionally with New Balance and made the World Championship team in 2015 and the World Indoor Championship team in 2016. However, in her build-up to the 2016 Olympic Trials, she suffered a stress fracture.

Abbey endured and made the 5000-meter final of the Olympic Trials. Despite Abbey's kick to the finish, history seemed to repeat itself, as she ended up in fifth pace, the same place she finished four years ago. This would mean she would miss out on an Olympic team berth. However, because first and second place finishers Molly Huddle and Emily Infeld opted to focus on the 10,000 meter, which they had qualified for earlier in the Trials, Abbey had made the Olympic team.

Finally an Olympian, Abbey ran the first 3 kilometers of the 5000-meter Olympic qualifying race focused, under control, and maintaining contact with the leaders. That's when disaster struck. Within a split second, Abbey was tripped by a woman who had fallen in front of her, causing the runner behind her to trip, and two runners, Abbey included, ended up on the ground.

A runner's first instinct after falling is usually to get up and sprint to catch up. But not Abbey. In a tremendous display of sportsmanship, she stopped to help and encourage the other fallen runner, New Zealand's Nikki Hamblin. At this point, it was clear the two runners were out of the race, but courageously wanted to finish. Despite obvious pain, Abbey tried to run as her knees continued to buckle. After the two runners finished and embraced, Abbey was wheeled off the track in a wheelchair.

The two runners were given the opportunity to run in the 5000-meter final, but an MRI showed that Abbey had torn the ACL, meniscus, and also suffered a strained MCL. Abbey demonstrated sportsmanship at the highest level. Her willingness to help a fellow competitor and the courage she displayed to finish the race despite a serious injury will be forever remembered as a great Olympic moment.

Questions For Thought:

1. Abbey used her failure as motivation. How have you used failure as motivation?
2. Abbey displayed tremendous courage to finish the Olympic race after a serious injury. What does the word courage mean to you?
3. How do you display good sportsmanship?

Andre De Grasse

A Lot Can Happen in Four Years

Andre De Grasse has been running competitively for just four years, but he's always been fast. His mother was a sprinter in high school when she lived in Trinidad and Tobago, before moving to Canada. But Andre gravitated towards basketball growing up and in his senior year in high school only two players came out for basketball. Two does not make a team and therefore Andre was looking for a new sport. He found track, running his first 100 meters in borrowed spikes, basketball shorts and from a standing start since he didn't know how to use starting blocks. The skinny little guy ran 10.9 and then went to his first track practice. In just two months, Andre dropped his time to 10.5 and received a scholarship to Coffeyville Community College in Kansas. At Coffeyville, he won five national titles and he was on his way to the University of Southern California.

USC was a dramatic change in his training. Drills and five a.m. workouts consisting of running hills made Andre a much improved sprinter. At the 2015 NCAA Outdoor Championships, he ran 9.75 to win the 100 and 19.58 to win the 200. Both would have smashed Canadian records but were wind-aided. He won a bronze at the 2015 IAAF Championships in the 100 to cap off his season. Just three and a half years removed from his first track meet, Andre turned pro and became a millionaire.

At 5 feet 9 inches tall and 154 pounds, Andre de Grasse lined up against Usain Bolt in the Olympic 100 meter final. Bolt at 6-5 and 207 pounds looked confident, like a multiple Olympic gold medalist should look. Andre looked as if he belonged in the Junior Olympics. But looks can be deceiving. Bolt won the race in 9.80 seconds, but Andre finished third in 9.91 seconds. He upped the medal color in the 200 meters, as he finished second behind Bolt in 20.02. He added a third Olympic medal in the 4 x 100 relay, anchoring the Canadians to bronze.

Only four years earlier, Andre had never ran track. A lot can happen in four years—three Olympic medals, the face of Canadian track and field, multi-million dollar professional contract, and heir apparent to succeed Usain Bolt as the world's fastest human.

Questions for Thought:

1. Andre committed to training hard and saw his times drop dramatically. How do you prepare before practice?
2. Looks can be deceiving. Looks do not guarantee a win. What is more important than looking good?
3. Andre has made dramatic improvements in his technique and mental game. How do the physical and the mental aspects work together?

Janay DeLoach

Making the Switch

Olympic glory came to Janay DeLoach in 2012 at the London Olympic Games with a bronze medal in the long jump. However, the next year, Janay broke her left foot, an injury that required two surgeries in 2014. In order to recover, she was required to keep weight off the foot for three months, causing her leg muscles to atrophy. Then, she tore her right quad.

Janay realized she would have to adapt so she switched her take-off foot from the left leg to the right leg. While it was new, it wasn't totally foreign to her, as she used her right leg to take off in the hurdles.

At the 2016 Olympic Trials in Eugene, Oregon, Janay fouled on her first two attempts. She was down to one final jump to deliver the goods to make her second Olympic team. She finally earned a mark on her third attempt, qualifying her for three more jumps in the finals. Before her last attempt, she sat in seventh place. However, Janay felt confident in her ability to rise to the occasion. Her training had prepared her for this moment, and she knew just how to calm herself down and trust in her abilities.

On her last attempt, she reached 22-9 to move into third place. She paced the sidelines and prayed as a handful of competitors continued to jump, awaiting the final results. No one else surpassed her, and Janay made her second-straight Olympic team.

Prior to the Trials, Janay had sprained her right ankle at a meet in Europe and the injury hadn't fully healed. She went into the Rio Olympics having not competed since the Trials. The injury caused her to just barely miss qualifying for the finals, finishing 13th when the top 12 advanced.

Through the tumultuous season and past couple of years, Janay plans to learn from her failures and do what it takes to return to the podium.

Questions For Thought:

1. Janay made a difficult transition when she switched take-off legs. Think of a transition you made. What made it difficult? How successful were you in making the transition?
2. Janay trains the mental component everyday to be able to respond under pressure. On a scale of 1-10, rate how well you prepare yourself mentally everyday.
3. How will your mental preparation prepare you to respond under pressure?

Genzebe Dibaba

Fast Family

Genzebe Dibaba comes from a family of some of the fastest runners on the planet.

The Dibaba sisters—seven of them—were raised in a tukul, or round mud hut. They had no electricity and survived on teff, barley, and wheat, all of which were products of their parents' subsistence farming. Their mother credits the siblings' success to the always-steady supply of milk from the family cows. Along with Kenya, Ethiopia lies in what some call an altitude sweet spot, around 6,000 to 9,000 feet, an altitude high enough to cause physiological changes but not too high so that it is too hard to train.

Her sisters and her are the only siblings in recorded history to hold concurrent world records. Tirunesh Dibaba is the most decorated of the siblings, with three Olympic gold medals. Their older sister, Ejegayehu, has a silver from Athens, and their cousin Derartu Tulu was the first black African woman to win an Olympic gold in the 1992 games. In her quest to join her family members as Olympic medalists, Genzebe was selected for the 2012 London Olympics, but was eliminated from competition due to a hamstring injury in the final lap of her opening round heat.

After breaking three world indoor records within two weeks in 2014, Genzebe dominated the competition in 2015. She set a world indoor 5000 meter record of 14:18.86 and then went unbeaten in her five 1500 meter races during the summer. She is the 1500-meter world record holder at 3:50.07.

She captured her first world outdoor title in Beijing in 2015, and won bronze in the 5000. She was named the 2015 female IAAF World Athletes of the Year. In 2016, she won the world indoor title in Portland at 3000 meters.

In Rio, Genzebe joined her sisters as Olympic medalists. Genzebe led through 1200 meters, but Kenya's Faith Kipyegon was close behind and took the lead with 200 meters to go. Genzebe ran 4:10.27 to take the silver medal in the 1500 meters.

Questions For Thought:

1. The Dibabas grew up without luxuries. How could that have contributed to their success?
2. The Dibaba family has a culture of excellence in distance running. What culture are you a part of?
3. How could you help establish a culture?

Ashton Eaton

World's Greatest Athlete

Ashton Eaton has ruled the decathlon since 2012.

Ashton was raised by a single mother in Oregon and she depended on coaches and teachers in Central Oregon to serve as male role models as Ashton grew up. At Mountain View High School in Bend, Oregon, Ashton was a multi-sport star in football, wrestling, and track and won state titles at 400 meters and the long jump. At the University of Oregon, he won three straight NCAA outdoor titles in the decathlon and two national titles in the indoor heptathlon, setting a world record in the heptathlon. Ashton set the decathlon world record in winning the 2012 U.S. Olympic Trials and followed up his world record performance by capturing his first Olympic gold medal in the decathlon. His performance included an Olympic decathlon record in the 100 meters, a season-best in the 110-meter hurdles, and a personal best in the javelin. Ashton continued the long, glorious tradition of U.S. decathletes winning Olympic gold.

Ashton saw an impressive winning streak in major events dating back to 2012, when he set the world record at the US Olympic Trials and went on to win his first Olympic gold medal in London. He collected two gold medals at the World Track and Field Championships and three more in the heptathlon at the World Indoor Championships. In 2015, Ashton broke his own decathlon world record by six points with a 9045-point total at the IAAF World Championships in Beijing.

At the 2016 Olympics, Ashton finished second behind Canadian Damian Warner in the first event of the day, the 100, but it was the only time in which a name other than Ashton Eaton would top the overall standings after an event. Ashton placed first in the long jump, first in the 400 meter, second in the 110-meter hurdles, and third in the pole vault. The final event came down to Ashton needing to finish no worse than seven seconds behind Frenchman Kevin Mayer in the 1500 meter to win the gold. He ended up finishing more than two seconds ahead of Mayer, securing the win. Though his total was off his own world record, it was enough to tie the Olympic record of 8893 points set in Athens in 2004.

Ashton joins track and field legends Bob Mathias from the U.S. and Daley Thompson of Great Britain as just the third man ever to repeat as Olympic champion in the decathlon. With back-to-back Olympic titles and the world record in the decathlon, Ashton Eaton has claimed the title of the world's greatest athlete.

Questions For Thought:

1. Training for the decathlon is time consuming. Are you willing to make sacrifices and put in the time it takes to get better?
2. Fatigue becomes a factor in the decathlon. How are you at managing fatigue?
3. Coach Harry Mara guides Ashton and his wife supports him. Who is on your support staff? How do you thank them?

Mo Farah

Double Doubler

Mo Farah has an gold Olympic medal for each of his children: dedicating Olympic gold medals to his twins, Amani and Aisha, and his eldest daughter, Rihanna. His final race of the 2016 Olympics, he promised one for his young son, Hussein, too. As usual, he delivered.

Mo Farah has always had a burning desire to be the best. In 2011, he relocated to Portland, Oregon to work with coach Alberto Salazar and train with Galen Rupp. Mo continued to improve with a breakthrough race in winning the gold medal in the 2011 World Championship 5000 meters and the silver at 10,000 meters. In the Summer 2012 Olympic Games, Mo delivered on the last lap of the 10,000 meter race. A week later, Mo also captured the Olympic 5000 meter gold. Mo, in his quest to be the best, had become a powerful emblem of London's diversity.

In the middle of the 2016 Olympic 10,000 meter final, it appeared as though his hopes to make history might be in danger. He got tangled up with American friend and training partner Galen Rupp, and crashed onto the track with 16 laps to go. The scene brought back memories for long-time track and field enthusiasts who remember Lasse Viren falling in the 1972 Olympic 10,000 final. Viren got up, kept his composure, and went on to win in world-record time. Mo's story had a similar ending. With enough time to recover and regain his composure, the race wasn't over for him and he got up to surge past the leader. With that race, he became the first British athlete ever to complete a hat-trick of Olympic gold medals. He wasn't done yet, though.

He achieved his fourth Olympic title in the same way as his other three, sitting at the back while waiting for the race to develop. With a lap to go, Mo had six athletes with him, but he ran his final lap in a speedy 52.83 seconds to win the 5000 meter in 13:03.30.

His 2016 Olympic victories made him only the second athlete to win the 5000 and 10,000 at two Olympic Games. Coincidentally, it was Lasse Viren, one of "the Flying Finns," who accomplished this in the Games of 1972 and 1976.

Questions For Thought:

1. Mo has established himself as one of the greatest distance runners in Olympic history. What can you learn from his story?
2. Mo often starts at the very back of the pack and works his way up. Do you always have a planned strategy?
3. When accidents happen, how do you keep your composure?

Allyson Felix

Most Decorated Olympic Medalist

The U.S. Olympic Trials were somewhat of a disappointment for American sprinter Allyson Felix. She was hoping to potentially become the third athlete to win gold in both the 200 and 400 at the Olympic Games. She was even instrumental in pushing for a scheduling change the International Olympic Committee granted in order to make the 200-400 double possible. While she was supposed to be cementing her track legacy at the Trials, she instead went into them limping, unsure, and hoping to qualify. After a freak incident while weight training, Allyson sustained an ankle injury which caused her to alter her training, including running the opposite way around the track, so as not to put as much strain on her right ankle.

The 200 is Allyson's specialty, one at which she's won three gold medals at world championships and a gold and two silvers at the Olympics. But at the U.S. Olympic Trials, she ended up outside of the top three, meaning she would not go on to run the race in Rio. She finished fourth, just .01 seconds behind the third-place finisher, Jenna Prandini. Although she did not go on to compete in her favorite race, she qualified in the 400 meters and was also a part of the 4x100 and 4x400 meter relay teams.

In Rio, the title she craved eluded her. She chased Shaunae Miller of the Bahamas down the homestretch but was denied her fifth Olympic gold medal by .07 seconds. Miller, who attended the University of Georgia and won the 2013 NCAA indoor title, plunged over the line with a dive. Felix ran 49.51 but came out second in the two-woman war.

Despite the disappointment, Felix claimed her seventh Olympic medal to become the most decorated female track and field athlete in history. Felix came away disappointed in the tough year where injuries derailed her 200-400 double gold dream. But considering all Allyson had to endure to even run, her sprint for a medal was remarkable.

Allyson would add another Olympic gold when she anchored the 4x400 relay team with a 49.66 split, as well as being a part of the gold medal winning 4x100 team.

Questions For Thought:

1. Allyson is capable of competing at a high level even when she is not at 100%. How tough are you to compete even when you are not at 100%?
2. Allyson takes great pride in giving her best. What pride do you have in putting forth your best effort?
3. Allyson is the most decorated female athlete in Olympic history. What successful traits does she possess that have allowed her to be a legend?

Mason Finley

Big Man- Big Throw

After spending three years on the Kansas University track and field team, Mason Finley transferred to Wyoming in 2012 after dealing with some family issues, saying he "just kind of had to get out of this area." Following his one year at Wyoming, his weight ballooned to 437 pounds. Along with the weight he lost flexibility and his ability to efficiently spin in the circle.

He made the decision to change his habits. He educated himself on better foods. He started doing workouts in the pool and his joints appreciated the lower impact. In three years, he lost 80 pounds. He began to train again with KU throwing coach Andy Kokhanovsky, who threw the discus for Ukraine at the 1996 Olympics in Atlanta. After a spinal injection for his ailing back, he had to take it easy. His only workouts were swimming for two months before he could get back into training. A year later, he set his personal record with a throw of 218-11 in the qualifying rounds of the U.S. Trials. The next day, his 208-1 in rainy conditions made him the U.S. champion and punched his ticket to Rio.

In Rio, he made the final with the sixth best qualifying throw but ran into a case of the nerves. Rather than having confidence in his training, he began to think too much about technique and had to settle for 11th place.

Mason's commitment to nutrition, technique and proper training has set himself up to be a factor in U.S. discus throwing for the next few Olympiads.

Questions For Thought:

1. Mason Finley used proper nutrition to improve performance. How can you educate yourself on proper nutrition?
2. In the Olympic final, nerves got to Mason. What are some techniques to focus on that may help control your nerves?
3. Mason was able to change his habits. How hard is it to change habits you have developed?

Shalane Flanagan

American Distance Legend

Shalane Flanagan grew up with the Boston Marathon basically in her backyard. She watched the elite runners go by at a pace faster than she could, at the time, even run for one mile.

At the University of North Carolina, she won two NCAA cross country titles and a NCAA Indoor 3000 meters title. She made her first Olympic team in the 5000 meters but did not advance from her heat at the 2004 Olympic Games. She didn't have her goals set on a medal, she was just happy to be there. With time, her goals and dreams, along with her training and experiences have evolved. She won the bronze medal in the 10,000 meters at the 2008 Olympics in Beijing and owns the second-fastest marathon time in American history with the 2:21:14 she clocked for third place at the 2014 Berlin Marathon.

With two big goals still on her bucket list, Shalane set out to accomplish them one at a time. The first—win the Boston marathon. The Boston Marathon adds a more emotional draw for Shalane than most. A win would be a way to honor her family, her hometown, and the nation that supports the Boston community. So far, she has finished fourth in 2013, seventh in 2014, and ninth in 2015. The second goal— another Olympic medal.

At the 2016 Olympic Marathon Trials, Shalane learned a valuable lesson. After leading the first 24 miles with teammate Amy Cragg, severe dehydration almost ended her chances of making her fourth Olympic team. Shalane had never competed in a marathon in conditions such as those in Los Angeles. Topping out at 73 degrees, it was the hottest Olympic Marathon Trials on record. She began to experience dizziness, chills, ringing in her ears, and blurred vision. Desiree Linden passed Shalane with about a mile to go, but fourth place finisher Kara Goucher was more than a minute behind. Shalane struggled with the last miles, but crossed the finish line and collapsed into Cragg's arms and was immediately taken to receive IV fluids. She had made her fourth Olympic team.

Shalane needed to properly hydrate for similar conditions in Rio. At the Trials, she only drank 2 to 4 ounces of fluid, and after seeing a hydration specialist, she was recommended to drink 10 to 14. In Rio, it was an 80-degree day, and Shalane made sure to properly hydrate in advance. Shalane Flanagan was the one who led the team of Americans to history with a sixth place in 2:25:06 with teammates Desiree Linden (2:26:08) and Amy Cragg (2:28:25) seventh and ninth, respectively, marking the USA's best team performance ever in the marathon.

Questions For Thought:

1. Shalane is always willing to learn. Do you continue to learn every day?
2. Over time, Shalane has evolved into one of the top runners in U.S. history. What are your long range goals as you evolve?
3. What's on your bucket list?

Courtney Frerichs

Big Dreamer

Growing up in Nixa, Missouri, Courtney Frerichs had dreams to go to the Olympics as a gymnast. Her early focus was on gymnastics but she eventually became a cross country and distance specialist and a triple jumper in high school. She continued her career at the University of Missouri-Kansas City and was introduced to the steeplechase. She finished sixth at the NCAA meet in the event as a sophomore. After sitting out the outdoor season as a junior, she was the NCAA runner-up as a senior. She went to graduate school at the University of New Mexico and under NCAA rules could compete and use her last year of eligibility. Courtney took full advantage of that opportunity, leading her team to an NCAA title in cross country and then winning the NCAA steeplechase championship with the best time in NCAA history.

Two weeks later, Courtney lined up in the final of the 3000-meter steeplechase with an opportunity to make the Olympic team. She needed a top three finish. Halfway through the race she ran in 7th place, and entering the final lap, she was in fourth. However, Courtney was up to the challenge. Her final lap was the fastest of all competitors as she moved into and finished in second place down the straightaway.

Courtney Frerichs had achieved her dream, not in gymnastics, but in track and field. And not in 2020, as she believed her Olympic time would come, but in 2016. Her performance at the Trials was the fourth-best time in U.S. history, running 9:20.92.

In Rio, Courtney became the 11th best runner in the world in an event she only knew existed for a relatively brief time. She finished in 9:22.87, just .14 seconds from a top-10 finish. Fellow American steeple chaser Emma Coburn became the first American to medal with a bronze in the event. Originally aiming for the 2020 Olympics in Tokyo, Courtney hopes to make the kind of leap Emma did from 2012 to 2016, as she went from 9th to 3rd.

She recently signed to run professionally with the Bowerman Track Club in Oregon, where she will move to train full-time and continue her Olympic dreams.

Questions For Thought:

1. Courtney had a dream and was willing to work to achieve it. Think of a dream you had that came true. Was it worth the effort?

2. Courtney has a strong finish. Even though she was seemingly out of contention for an Olympic team spot on the final lap she summoned the courage to dig down. Think of when you dug down deep and the results paid off.

3. Courtney ran at a small high school but had big dreams. Do you dream big? What kind of plan do you have to achieve your dreams?

English Gardner

Baby Beast

English Gardner was a freshman in high school and already an accomplished sprinter when she learned her mother was fighting stage four breast cancer. English's only release was track practice—those two hours each day where she didn't have to think about her family struggles.

During a charity powder-puff football game during her junior year in high school, English nearly ended her track career when she tore her ACL, MCL, and meniscus. These injuries cost her two years of high school competition and caused her to miss out on every college scholarship offer she had accrued except for the University of Oregon.

At Oregon, English won five NCAA championships. After her success in college, English decided to take on the 2012 summer Olympics in London. Knowing her mother had beaten the odds, Gardner planned to do the same in 2012. She was 20 years old and ready to conquer the world, ready to upset a field full of pros and make her first Olympic team. English finished a disappointing seventh place in the 100 meter at the 2012 trials, and she wasn't even invited into the U.S. relay pool.

Four years later, English was back at Hayward Field, running again for a spot on Team USA. Though English was oozing with confidence at the starting line, she had spent most of her pre-race routine throwing up, crippled with anxiety. She had been battling depression and anxiety for seven months prior to the Trials. The downward spiral began with a failed romantic relationship, and she began to have doubts about her goals and destiny on the track. She lost weight, began taking sleep aides for insomnia, and her training went downhill.

When the gun sounded at the 2016 Trials, English channeled her alter ego she had created to help calm her anxiety and mask the fear. "Baby Beast" is a side of English that is serious, confident, and unafraid. Though it was a new Olympic year, she had to find a way to keep the thoughts of 2012 from returning. But unlike in 2012, she roared across the line in the 100-meter finals in 10.74, earning a new personal best and a spot on the Olympic team, overcoming the anxiety that had ruled her life for months.

In Rio, English missed out on a medal and finished in seventh, but captured the gold in the 4x100 meter relay along with teammates Tianna Bartoletta, Allyson Felix, and Tori Bowie.

Questions For Thought:

1. English had a devastating knee injury could have ended her career. What does "the greater the challenge, the greater the reward" mean to you?
2. What techniques can you use to handle anxiety and be successful?
3. When your confident level dwindles, what techniques can you use to increase your confidence?

Justin Gatlin

Chasing Away the Past

Justin Gatlin has been chasing Usain Bolt for more than a decade, but he's also been chasing down and trying to run away from a past haunted by doping accusations. As the 34-year-old entered the Olympic Stadium in Rio to run the 100-meter final, boos filled the stadium.

Gatlin has seen three Olympic Games and has earned a medal of every color. He was suspended in 2001 for testing positive for a substance in Adderall, an attention deficit disorder medication. The term, originally two years, was reduced to one year. He won gold in the 2004 Olympic Games in the 100 meter, bronze in the 200 meter, and silver in the 4x100 meter relay. After Bolt burst onto the scene, Gatlin was left behind. He served a four-year ban from 2006 to 2010 after testing positive for testosterone. He returned in 2012 to win bronze in the 100 meter and silver in the 4x100 meter relay. Though several years removed from the ban, Gatlin spent the next several years fighting off Bolt and the critics.

In 2014 and 2015, Gatlin ran six of the year's seven fastest 100-meter times in both years. He went undefeated from the final race of the 2013 season to the 100-meter final at the IAAF World Championships in Beijing. But Bolt peaked on the biggest stage, claiming the 100-meter gold at the 2015 World Championships, leaving Gatlin with silver medals in the 100 and 200.

Gatlin became the oldest U.S. sprinter to reach the Olympic Games since 1912 in the 100 meter after winning in 9.80 seconds, the second-fastest time run in the history of the U.S. Olympic Trials. He held off LaShawn Merritt in the final strides to clench the 200-meter Olympic Trials title from lane eight in 19.75 seconds.

In Rio, the five-time Olympic medalist failed to advance to the 200-meter final. Gatlin finished third in his heat after he let up prematurely, missing an automatic qualifying spot by .03 seconds. But his first round 100 looked effortless. In the 100-meter final, Gatlin was aiming to regain the title he won in 2004. Bolt was slower out of the blocks than Gatlin, but surged ahead around 60 meters to pass Gatlin. With his silver medal, Gatlin became the oldest man to ever win an Olympic track medal.

Questions For Thought:

1. Justin Gatlin has dealt with criticism, but continues to fight for his dream. How do you deal with and look past criticism?
2. Other athletes have been served sentences for banned substances, but haven't faced nearly as much backlash. What can you do to prove your doubters wrong?
3. Since the first modern Olympic Games in 1896, the average 100 meter gold medalist has been 23 years old. How can you use your age, young or old, to your advantage?

Andrea Geubelle

Jumping to Success

Andrea Geubelle is fueled by adversity. She loves to take a negative experience and turn it into a motivational factor.

The former University of Kansas three-time NCAA Division I triple jump champion thought she had won the NCAA outdoor triple jump title in 2012 when she was called away by a meet official and told that an opposing coach had protested that her winning jump was a foul, taking her from first to third. That same year, Andrea finished third at the U.S. Olympic Trials but had missed the Olympic qualifying standard by a mere centimeter and therefore could not go to London.

Rather than hang up the spikes, she used these experiences to inspire her. She won her second consecutive indoor NCAA title in 2013 and won the USA Outdoor Championship in 2013. But she spent most of the last year and a half trying to rehabilitate a torn patella tendon in her right knee. It bothered her to the point where she thought about giving up the sport. She would have conversations with friends and family about walking away, but she never walked far.

Rather than having surgery to repair the knee, she underwent prolotherapy — an alternative-medicine treatment that involves injections and painful physical therapy. Because the muscles around her kneecap were still not at full strength, Andrea had to alter her jumping style.

Because Andrea had met the IAAF qualifying standard (46-5 ¼) at a meet she won earlier in the summer, all she needed to do was finish in the top three at the trials in Eugene. At the Olympic Trials, she jumped 45-9 ¼ on her second-to-last attempt in the finals to grab the third and final qualifying spot for the Olympics.

At the Olympic Games, Andrea Geubelle was unable to finish among the top-12 in order to advance to the finals, but saved her best attempt for last in the qualifying rounds, eventually finishing 21st with a mark of 46-8 ½.

Questions For Thought:

1. Andrea's attitude has allowed her to overcome setbacks. How does your attitude determine your altitude?
2. Andrea has had to adapt. Are you able to adapt to meet the situation?
3. Do you enjoy what you do? Is enjoyment a factor in your success?

Kate Grace

Finally an Olympic Finalist

Kate Grace was a dark horse in the 800 meters at the 2016 US Olympic Trials. After a misfortune of events for two of the top three runners in the event, Kate was in fourth with 150 meters to go. She then sprinted down the homestretch to win in 1:59.10.

As a Yale Bulldog, Kate qualified for multiple NCAA National Championships in both the 800 and 1500 meters and became a four-time All-American. She flew under the radar and had five frustrating and injury-riddled professional seasons after she graduated from Yale. In 2013 planter fasciitis cut into her season and in 2015 she was immobilized for two months after suffering a torn ligament in her toe.

Oiselle, a Seattle-based woman's running and fitness apparel company, had taken on Kate as their first sponsored athlete at the beginning of her professional career. Her win at the Trials was a major victory for the corporate sponsor and they wanted to celebrate accordingly. Oiselle posted a photo to social media of Kate clutching an American flag next to a quote after her race. An U.S. Olympic Committee official told the company to take down all photos of Kate and other Oiselle athletes competing at the Trials from the company's social media platforms and to stop all "Olympic-related advertising."

Despite the controversy, Kate had other worries after she ran her semi-final heat of the 800 in Rio. Though she finished with a personal best of 1:58.79, she finished third in her heat, and only the top two would automatically qualify so she had to rely on getting in on time. With three heats remaining, she was sitting with the seventh-best time when the top eight would go on—but she squeaked in.

Starting in lane one, Kate had a tough go at it from the beginning. She was quickly boxed in and fell to the back of the pack, causing her to adjust her race strategy. Unfortunately, Kate did not have the same kick down the homestretch characteristic of her past performances and ended in eighth with a time of 1:59.57.

Questions For Thought:

1. Despite limited success, Kate persisted and eventually succeeded. Rate your level of persistence on a scale of 1 to 10 (1=low, 10=high).
2. How can your mental skills help you handle frustration?
3. Kate races patiently and then finishes strong. How do you finish what you start?

Gabriele Grunewald

Overcoming the Odds

Gabriele Grunewald was diagnosed with cancer at the age of 22. Then again at 24. She never dreamed of becoming a professional runner with the prospect of being an Olympian. She definitely didn't dream of doing it after her second diagnosis with cancer.

Gabriele, or "Gabe," was first diagnosed with adenoid cystic carcinoma in 2009 when she was a fifth-year senior at the University of Minnesota. After surgery and treatment, she asked the NCAA for a medical hardship waiver to run in the 2010 outdoor season. Her sixth year on the team, she went on to become the NCAA runner-up in the 1500. The year following her initial diagnosis was a breakthrough year for Gabe as a runner.

In 2010, Gabe was derailed by a diagnosis with thyroid cancer, unrelated to her first cancer diagnosis. Since her recovery from her second bout with cancer, she has finished fourth in the 1500 at the 2012 U.S. Olympic Track & Field Trials, lowered her 1500-meter personal best to 4:01.48, and won the 2014 USA Indoor 3000-meter title.

At the U.S. Olympic Trials in July 2016, Gabe unexpectedly failed to advance to the final of the 5000 meter, so she ran the 1500 meter less than two hours after the 5000 prelim. She advanced to the finals, where she finished 12th.

In early August, her husband, who is a third-year resident physician in internal medicine, noticed her abdomen felt unusual when he hugged her. She had felt an unusual tightness in her rib cage, but she thought it was a running-related ache from her diaphragm or a tight core muscle. That evening, a CT scan revealed a large tumor, a metastatic recurrence of her first cancer—her third cancer diagnosis.

Just a month after running in the Olympic Trials with an unknown cancerous tumor in her liver, Gabe underwent surgery to make her a three-time cancer survivor.

After the surgery, Gabe posted on social media, "A journey of a thousand miles begins with a single step." Her cancer diagnosis led her to question whether or not she would continue her running career, but she ultimately decided she isn't finished yet—the 2020 Olympics are still in her sights and she's already proven she can defeat anything in her way.

Questions For Thought:

1. Gabe never gives up. Do you?
2. Gabe's strong, positive attitude has been vital factor to her success. How do you keep yourself positive under challenging circumstances?
3. How are you doing on your journey of 1000 miles?

Kendra Harrison

From Disappointment to World Record

Kendra "Keni" Harrison went from the lowest point in her career to the highest point within a matter of weeks. After finishing a disappointing sixth place in the 2016 Olympic Trials and failing to make the team, she and the rest of the world were shocked considering she broke the American record just a few weeks prior at the Prefontaine Classic in the summer of 2016.

The day after the Trials final, Keni and her coach were back at the track, doing her least-favorite workout: 10 hurdles, twice through. Her thoughts went from being 'only the sixth best hurdler in the nation' to those of being a 'great hurdler that had a bad day on the worst possible day' during the workout that day.

Heading into the London Diamond League 100-meter hurdle race, Keni was still recovering from the Trials heartbreak. When she crossed the line in 12.40 ahead of the field during the preliminary race, she finally smiled and let go of the past. In the finals, Keni faced all three athletes who made the U.S. team and carried American flags just weeks prior. Nia Ali was in lane five, Keni in lane six, Brianna Rollins in lane seven, and Kristi Castlin in lane nine. By the third hurdle, Keni had a lead on the field.

Just moments before the race, Keni's coach had told her to lean. She didn't know why—he had said this race is going to be special. When she leaned at the line, she was well ahead of the field but the clock showed her winning time as 12.57. But Keni had leaned so low that she dipped underneath the beam and the clock didn't register her time right away. It wasn't until the clock was corrected that Keni saw she had broken the world record with a time of 12.20, breaking Yordanka Donkova's 1988 world record by one hundredth of a second.

Keni Harrison faced tough competition and had an off day at the worst time. However, the measure of a great athlete is to bounce back.

Questions For Thought:

1. Keni did not wallow in pity or feel sorry for herself. How quickly do you bounce back after adversity?
2. What do you do after adversity?
3. What mental skills do you have to allow yourself to release the negative thoughts of past performances?

Jeff Henderson

Promises, Promises

Long jumper Jeff Henderson's coach knows how to win. Al Joyner, his coach and 1984 Olympic triple jump gold medalist, motivated Jeff the same way he motivated his wife, the late Florence Griffith Joyner. Al gave Jeff his 1984 gold medal in Rio and told him before the competition, "Give back my gold medal and you keep your gold medal." He did the same with FloJo, and she went on to win both the 100 and 200 meter at the Seoul 1988 Olympic Games. Henderson was confident that he didn't need Al's gold medal—he could earn his own. He believed in himself so much that gave the gold medal back before he even stepped on the track.

And he knew the minute he landed that he had his own gold medal to keep. On his sixth and final attempt, Jeff jumped a season best 27-6 to clench the gold by one of the narrowest victories at the Rio Games, just one centimeter.

Jeff likes to make promises. He dedicated his gold medal to his mother, Debra, who was diagnosed with Alzheimer's disease 10 years ago. He had promised to win a gold medal for her before he left, and he made good on that promise during an emotional homecoming to his hometown of McAlmont, Arkansas, where his mother has been bedridden since he was 17 years old.

Jeff's goal is to go after the world record in the long jump, a challenge he relishes since he ranks among some of the best long jumpers in history. His gold was the first for Team USA since Dwight Phillips in 2004. Carl Lewis won a record four straight long jump gold medals from 1984 to 1996.

Questions For Thought:

1. Jeff's coach has a gold medal himself and coached his wife to two gold medals at the 1988 Olympics, and used that to motivate Jeff. Who motivates you?
2. Just one centimeter separated gold and silver at the Rio Games. What can you do to make sure you're going the distance to succeed?
3. When you make promises, do you follow through with them?

Molly Huddle

Lesson Learned

You probably won't see Molly Huddle celebrate much at the finish line. Molly was set to win the bronze medal at the 2015 World Championships in Beijing. But she let up just a little too early, raising her arms in the air in celebration, and teammate Emily Infeld surged past to finish .09 seconds ahead of her and take the bronze. Huddle said it would "take a long time to get over," but it was a lesson learned.

When Molly became the first woman to win both the 5000 and 10,000 U.S. Olympic Trials titles, all she could do was smile.

Molly graduated from Elmira Notre Dame High School in 2002, where she won multiple state championships in cross country and track, went undefeated and finished fourth in the Foot Locker Nationals Her school did not have a cross country program, so Molly did not run cross country until her senior year, when her father coached her as a one-person team. At the University of Notre Dame, she was a 10-time All-American. Molly began establishing herself as one of the top talents in collegiate distance running by finishing seventh in the 5000 meters at the 2004 U.S. Olympic Trials.

After qualifying for the 2008 Olympic Trials, a nagging calf injury held Molly to a ninth place finish in the 10,000 meters and a 10th place finish in the 5000 meters. She finished 11th in the 5000 at the 2012 Olympic Games.

In Rio, Ethiopia's Almaz Ayana set a blistering world-record pace early on and went on to shatter the 23-year-old world record, finishing in 29:17.45. Molly finished in 30:13.17 for sixth place for a bittersweet ending, with an American record but no Olympic medal.

The pace was torrid from the start and although Molly had gone through the halfway point in 14:55 and was well on her way to the race of her life, she had already lost contact with the leaders. Her time would have earned her a medal at every previous Olympic Games and gold at six out of seven of them. Eight runners set national records in this race. Molly Huddle's time cut more than 9 seconds from the American Record Shalane Flanagan set at the 2008 Olympic Games.

Questions For Thought:

1. Molly let up at the finish line of the World Championships and it cost her a medal. Do you always finish strong, all the way through to the finish?
2. Molly was the only member of her girls cross country team but pushed herself to succeed. How do you challenge yourself when the conditions are less than ideal?
3. Molly put her mistakes behind her and moved on. How do you put your mistakes behind you and learn from them?

Caterine Ibargüen

Golden History

The nation of Colombia had won only three medals in their Olympic history, and going into the Rio 2016 Olympic Games, Colombia's Caterine Ibargüen was their biggest hope for a gold medal.

Growing up, Caterine's parents worked on local plantations and she grew up on a diet rich in bananas and fish. The family survived on a meager income. Amid escalating conflicts between guerrillas and paramilitary groups during the Colombian Conflict, Caterine's parents separated when she was seven. She was then raised by her grandmother, who often struggled to put food on the table.

Caterine's natural athletic attributes were evident from an early age. At the age of 14, she was sent to Medellin, Colombia's second largest city, to train under a succession of Cuban coaches, focusing on the high jump. She won her first medal, a bronze, at the senior South American Championships in Bogota in 1999 at age 15.

Caterine continued to win medals at various South American championships, but failing to qualify for the 2008 Beijing Olympics resulted in depression and she almost quit the sport. She decided to change careers and accepted a scholarship to compete for the Metropolitan University of Puerto Rico and study nursing.

However, under the guidance of a new coach, she was persuaded to continue but focus solely on the triple jump.

She came out of the London 2012 Olympics with a triple jump of 48-6 and a silver medal. In 2013, Caterine made Colombian history by winning gold at the World Championships in Moscow, a feat she then repeated in Beijing at the 2015 Championships.

The two-time world champion was the favorite going into the Rio Games after winning 36 of her last 37 competitions excluding qualifying events. With a triple jump of 49-0 ¼, Caterine Ibargüen claimed Colombia's first Olympic gold medal in track and field.

Questions For Thought:

1. Caterine has had ups and downs in her career. How do you get through the downs to get to the ups?
2. A difficult childhood led to mental toughness and a strong will. On a scale of 1-10, rate your willpower.
3. Caterine was the favorite and came through when it counted. What are your thoughts focused on when you know you are the favorite?

Evan Jager

Running Relaxed

Four years prior, Evan Jager had spent the months leading up to the Olympic Games full of nerves. His life centered around the Olympics and the chance to compete, but when it came time to perform, the end result was a disappointing 6th place in the 3000-meter steeplechase. At the IAAF World Championships in Beijing in 2015, Evan had the fastest time in the world for the year, but once again finished 6th. The pattern caused Evan to re-evaluate his approach to races. He needed to relax more and think less.

On July 4, 2015 at the Paris Diamond League meet, Evan was in a steeplechase field that included the world's top steeplechasers. He overtook each runner over the course of the final lap and it appeared he was on his way to winning, breaking his own American record, and his first sub-8:00. But when Evan's foot brushed the top of the barrier, he fell to the track. He got up immediately, but succumbed the lead. He came up just short of a sub-8:00 clocking, running 8:00.45—more than four seconds off his previous American record of 8:04.71.

He spent time leading up to the Olympics clearing his conscience and trying to release his nerves. He prepared to treat the Olympic Games just as he would any other training session. All he could tell himself to do was, "relax, relax."

The 27-year-old Illinois native got to the front early in the 2016 Olympic steeplechase final, setting a fast pace in order to distance himself and the leaders from the rest of the field. With just four laps to go, Evan took the lead to keep the race in his hands and control. It wasn't a pre-calculated plan of attack, but rather what he felt he needed to do in that moment. Evan, along with Kenya's Conseslus Kipruto and Ezekiel Kemboi of Kenya, had broken away from the pack. By the final lap, Kipruto sprinted ahead of Evan and Kemboi, turning it into a race for silver. Evan passed Kemboi around 100 meters to go.

In what he described as a "perfect race," Evan won the United States' first medal in the men's event since Brian Diemer's bronze in 1984, capturing silver and finishing in a time of 8:04.28. It was highest finish for an American since Horace Ashenfelter won gold in 1952. Evan Jager's time would have been an Olympic record had it not been for Kipruto, who took gold in 8:03.28.

Questions For Thought:

1. Evan underperformed when he was a bundle of nerves. What techniques do you use to relax before a competition?
2. Evan beat out Kemboi, the two-time gold medalist, who is considered by many to be the best steeplechase runner ever. What kind of confidence does it take to race against the best in the world?
3. What does your "perfect race" look like?

Charles Jock

Running to Survive

Charles Jock was born into a family on the run. South Sudan's second civil war chased his parents into Ethiopia, where Jock was born in the capital, Addis Ababa. The family wasn't allowed to stay, and returned to Sudan, but were forced to leave again, beginning a yearlong trek across deserts, jungles, and mountains. At the age of three, Charles Jock was trudging behind his parents—walking until sunset, eating what they could forage, and simply running away to survive.

After bouncing around from refugee camp to refugee camp, Jock eventually made it to the United States to begin a new journey: as a middle distance runner. It was a relief after the early part of his life, but his new path was not without its difficulties. Jock was one of the favorites in the 2012 Olympic Trials after coming off the 800 meter NCAA championship running for the University of California Irvine, but his Olympic dream faded on the backstretch as he battled hamstring pain and went from the lead to last.

That finish made his 2016 Olympic Trials result redemptive. He was once again dealing with a hamstring injury, but things went his way this time. The 26-year-old was running second to last with 200 meters to go but a strong finish propelled him to third place with a time of 1:45.48 to qualify for the U.S. Olympic team.

In Rio, Jock failed to qualify out of the opening heats. He ran from the back of the pack, and by the time he made his move with 150 to go, it was too late, as he finished seventh in heat 4 in 1:47.06.

Charles Jock's journey from Sudan to Ethiopia to the United States and to compete at the world's largest athletic stage in Rio has been challenging to say the least. His commitment to a dream has inspired countless athletes to reach their goals.

Questions for Thought:

1. Charles Jock is a survivor. He has not only survived but thrived. How can you overcome obstacles to thrive?
2. Think of all the things you take for granted in your life.
3. How can you be thankful of your environment and support system?

Meb Keflezighi

Marathon Mebrahtom

Meb Keflezighi crossed the finish line of the 2016 Olympic Marathon in Rio in a disappointed 33rd place after miles of dry heaving and throwing up. He had already claimed it would be his last Olympics. One might think after having to stop seven times throughout marathon number 24, Meb would call it quits. But he still has two more marathons left to run in order to live up to his full name, Mebrahtom, which sounds like marathon, to make it an even 26 for his career.

Meb is the only athlete in history to win the New York Marathon, the Boston Marathon and an Olympic Medal. He won a silver medal in the Marathon at the 2004 Olympics in Athens, he was the 2009 ING New York City Marathon champion, and the 2014 Boston Marathon champion. He also has four NCAA championships from his time at the University of California Los Angeles, 22 National Championships and a place on three United States Olympic teams.

Meb finished second behind Galen Rupp at the 2016 Olympic Trials in Los Angeles, running 2:12:20, taking 1 minute, 12 seconds off the U.S. Masters marathon record he set in 2015. With this finish, he became the oldest American to make the Olympic marathon team. At 41 years old, cramps bothered him until mile 14 or 15 at the Trials, but would get the best of him in Rio.

Overcome by stomach problems, Meb stopped as early as at the 13 mile mark and would continue to stop six more times to either dry heave or vomit, including once right before entering the race's final straightaway. Meb finished in 33rd place in 2:16:46, far behind the winner, Eliud Kipchoge of Kenya, and Americans Galen Rupp and Jared Ward. Rupp was the bronze medalist in 2:10:05 and Ward was sixth in 2:11:30. Just as Meb was crossing the finish line, he slipped in a puddle and fell to the ground. Just for good measure, he threw in a few pushups before getting up and crossing the finish line, which was just inches from his nose.

Though his Olympic career is over, Meb's success has come from being persistent in pursuit of his dreams. "Never give up on your dreams. Some dreams might come early, some dreams might come at 40 or 41, so keep being persistent."

Questions For Thought:

1. Meb wants to run 26 marathons in his career. What long range goals do you have?
2. Meb has made history for several of his accomplishments. What do you want to be remembered for?
3. According to Meb, the key to success is persistency. Are you persistent in your goals?

Sam Kendricks

Proud American

Sam Kendricks is a proud American. The former Ole Miss track star is a second lieutenant in the U.S. Army Reserve. An event that illustrated his extreme patriotism happened as he was competing in the qualifying round at the Rio Olympic Games. He was running down the pole vault runway preparing to plant his pole into the vault box when he heard the national anthem begin to play. He suddenly stopped his approach run, dropped his vaulting pole and stood at attention.

Sam competed as a track and field athlete throughout his high school years in Oxford, Mississippi. He loved to run the relays, but eventually gravitated to pole vaulting when he found out that was his strength.

When Sam went to the University of Mississippi, he joined the Army ROTC. The level of excellence that the Army ROTC demonstrated fit Sam's desires and he immediately felt at home and comfortable. He began to thrive, motivated by the stress of competing. Sam maintains that, the more pressure there is, the better he performs—he thrives on it.

Army 2nd Lt. Sam Kendricks won the men's pole vault and secured a spot on the U.S. Olympic team at the Olympic Track and Field Trials.

At the 2016 Olympic Trials conditions during the preliminary and final rounds were hot and windy. Though those elements may be difficult to compete in, they are similar to those of Oxford, Mississippi, where Sam lives and trains.

Sam has practiced for years in wind and rain and was properly prepared for all conditions. "I have been to meets where it has rained; the wind has been directly in your face or to the side and that makes it very difficult." Sam's philosophy is that "the pole vault is favored by the man who is the most hardy jumper because he can jump in all conditions."

Sam cleared the bar at 19-4 ¾ inches, an Olympic trials record that set the prelude to his bronze medal in Rio.

Sam Kendricks won the bronze in the Olympic final of the men's pole vault, an event that was delayed by rain, with a jump of 19 feet 2 ¼ inches, becoming the first American to medal in the event in 12 years.

Questions For Thought:

1. Sam is proud of his country. What do you do to demonstrate your patriotism?
2. Sam is ready for all conditions. How do you prepare for that physically?
3. How do you prepare mentally to compete in all conditions?

Joe Kovacs

Throwing Out of the Parking Lot Ring

On the road to Rio, Joe Kovacs encountered much heartbreak. At a young age, Joe lost his father to colon cancer. Just hours later, his grandmother passed away of heart failure. "It was sad losing my father and him not being there, but my mom stepped up so much and provided so much for me," he says. "It was never, 'look down upon yourself,' it was always 'keep looking forward.'

Joe began throwing in a parking lot in high school, with his mom as his coach. He didn't have a track or a throwing circle, so they went out to the parking lot, and started drawing chalk lines. He eventually became good enough to earn a scholarship to Penn State University.

At the 2012 U.S. Olympic Trials, in his last meet wearing a Penn State jersey, Kovacs stood in third place in the standings, the final qualifying position for the London Games, after his third of six throws. However, 2009 World champion Christian Cantwell jumped ahead of Kovacs, who would finish in fourth place, one spot shy of becoming the youngest American to make the Olympics in the event in 20 years. Still, Kovacs had thrown a personal best at the biggest meet of his life, coming in with no expectations of cracking the top three.

Joe represented Team USA in the 2015 World Championships and won a gold medal with a record throw of 71-11 ½. Kovacs trained at the U.S. Olympic Training Center at Chula Vista with Olympic teammates Ryan Crouser and Darrell Hill. His training included gymnastic movements such as high bar swings and front and back handsprings.

Kovacs took 2nd at the 2016 Olympic Trials shot put, throwing 72-0 ¼ behind Ryan Crouser's lifetime best of 72-6 ½.

Joe took the early lead in the Olympic final throwing 71-5 ½, which would prove to be his best throw and good enough to capture the silver medal after teammate Crouser's Olympic record.

Questions For Thought:

1. Joe suffered family tragedy with the loss of loved ones, but continued to look forward. How do you see past your problems to the future?
2. Joe's mom adapted by creating a ring out of a parking lot. Think of a story where you overcame the odds.
3. Joe finished only one spot out of the Olympic team in 2012 and worked harder to make the team in 2016. What are some things you have learned from failing?

Erik Kynard

Chasing the American Record

In high school, Erik Kynard's dream was to compete in the high jump at the Olympics. Erik found success in high jumping at an early age. He cleared 7-0 by the age of 15 and qualified for the 2008 Olympic Trials as a 17-year-old high school athlete, and four years later, he made his dream come true, winning the silver medal at the London Olympic Games. As a high school senior at Rogers High School in Toledo, Ohio, Erik was a two-time Ohio state champion in the high jump and won both the 2009 Nike Outdoor and Indoor Championships in the high jump with clearances of 7-3 ¼ and 7-3. Erik took his high jumping skills to Kansas State University to compete under the tutelage of high jump guru coach Cliff Rovelto. During his freshman year at Kansas State, he posted a season best of 7-3 ¾ to finish second at the Big 12 Indoor Championships. He improved dramatically as a sophomore by winning the NCAA Outdoor Championships and then placed third at the USA Outdoor Championships, earing a right to compete in the World Championships in Daegu, South Korea. Erik added NCAA champion in 2011 and 2012 to his collegiate resume at K-State.

Over the last Olympiad, Erik Kynard has continued to prove why he is the top high jumper in the United States and one of the top high jumpers in the world. Erik has not only worked on his physical preparation, but he has also focused on improving his mental game and his preparing to lead a successful life. At just 21 years old during the London Olympic Games, Erik proved both his ability in the high jump and his composure by securing silver. In 2013, he claimed his first USA Outdoor Championship in addition to becoming one of only seven American men to ever clear 7-9 ¼. In 2014, Erik won his first USA Indoor title.

In the Rio Games, Erik had his sights set on moving up one spot to take the gold. In a tightly contested high jump battle, Erik cleared 7-7 ¾ but Derek Drouin of Canada cleared 7-10 ½ to take the gold and Erik finished in sixth. Though he jumped the same height as the bronze medallist, he had more misses.

With a personal record of 7-9 ¼, Erik is only one inch short of the American record of 7-10 ¼ set by Charles Austin in 1991. With consistency in his physical and mental preparation, Erik continues to strive to be the best high jumper in the world, a dream he has had since youth.

Questions For Thought:

1. Erik has been very consistent at placing in big meets. What type of physical and mental preparation does take to be consistent?
2. Erik has used the motivation of a second place Olympics to get better, yet he has not become obsessed with winning the gold. How do you keep your goals in proper perspective?
3. Erik has focused on improving in life as well as athletics. What goals do you have to improve in life?

Bernard Lagat

Five Time Olympian

In his long and storied track and field career, Bernard Lagat has gained a reputation around the world for his track and field excellence and the class manner in which he conducts himself. The 41-year-old Bernard Lagat made history as the oldest American ever to run at an Olympic Games.

In the U.S. Olympic Trials, Bernard came from behind to pass 5 runners in the last lap, some 15 years his junior, running 52.82 for the final 400 meters of the men's 5000-meter to win the Trials. Lagat said after the race, according to Sports Illustrated, "If you believe that you're old, you're going to run like an old man."

Bernard made his first Olympic appearance at the 2000 Olympics in Sydney where he won a bronze medal for his native Kenya. In 2004 he took home a silver medal in the 1500-meter. Then in 2008, he made his first Olympics appearance for the U.S. (where he moved to attend college at Washington State) at the games in Beijing with a disappointing ninth place finish in the 5000-meter. He competed for the U.S. again in London in 2012 with a fourth place finish in the 5000.

In his fifth Olympic Games, Bernard came home in sixth place in a respectable 13:06.78, a season best for the 5000 meter race.

Bernard Lagat will go down in history as one of the all-time greats. The second fastest 1500-meter runner of all time, he holds American records at 1500 and the mile indoors and the 1500, 3000 and 5000 outdoors.

Questions for Thought:

1. What has contributed to Bernard Lagat's longevity?
2. Bernard has a reputation of being a class act. What characteristics do you think make up a class act?
3. Bernard believes that he is still young and competes like it. How important is the mind in controlling the body?

Renaud Lavillenie

Vaulting Victories

Heading into the Olympics, Renaud Lavillenie was the world record holder at 20-2 ½, had won 19 of 25 competitions in 2015 and 15 of 17 competitions in 2016, and won the gold medal in London in 2012. He had won two World Indoor Championships gold medals, three European Championships gold medals and four European Indoor Championships gold medals. He had also won one silver medal and two bronze medals at the World Championships and held the French national records for the highest pole vault clearance both outdoors (19-10 ¼) and indoors (20-2 ½). He has been the pole vault overall winner of the IAAF Diamond League in six consecutive years, from 2010 to 2015.

But no man had repeated as Olympic champion in the men's pole vault since the U.S.'s Bob Richards in 1956. Needless to say, Renaud was the favorite to win the gold medal.

The treatment Renaud received from the crowd in Rio was shocking. The crowed booed Renaud on his final attempt at 19-9 ¼, a height Brazilian rival Thiago Braz da Silva cleared on his second attempt. Renaud reacted to the crowd with a thumbs-down gesture before subsequently missing the attempt and securing the gold for Da Silva. The crowd again booed before Renaud received his silver medal, leaving the Frenchman in tears on the podium during the Brazilian national anthem.

Immediately after the competition, Renaud had compared his treatment to that of Jesse Owens in the 1936 Olympics in Berlin, the black American athlete whose historic four gold medals were an affront to the Nazi regime's ideology on race, though he later withdrew the comments and apologized. Renaud admitted he was humiliated by the actions of the crowd and believed it to be a lack of fair play.

Questions For Thought:

1. Renaud is recognized as one of the top vaulters in history yet he felt disrespected in Rio. How important is good sportsmanship to you?
2. What do you do to display good sportsmanship?
3. What can you do to make the sport of track and field better?

Jarrion Lawson

Handing It To 'Em

Jarrion Lawson was a 15-time All-American at the University of Arkansas. Jarrion made history in 2016, joining Jesse Owens as the only athlete in American history to complete a rarity at the NCAA track and field championships, winning the 100 (10.22), 200 (20.19), and long jump (26-9) at the same meet. His 31.5 total points at the meet are also the most by an athlete since Owens' performance 80 years ago in 1935-36.

As a student at Arkansas, Jarrion completed his undergraduate degree in kinesiology in only three years before turning his attention to getting a master's in business administration in his fourth year of eligibility. Jarrion put as much emphasis developing his mind in graduate school as he did honing his leaping skills on the runway. He holds a 4.0 grade point average in MBA coursework. Prior to his standout collegiate career, Lawson was a five-time Texas state champion on the track at Liberty-Eylau High School and also lettered and captained the school's basketball and football teams.

Jarrion, a native of Texarkana, Texas, is a six-time national champion following a trio of wins, adding to two championships in the indoor long jump in 2014 and 2016 and one as part of the outdoor 4x100 relay in 2015.

In Rio, Jarrion was sitting in contention with a 27-0 ¾ jump. His last jump could have catapulted him to the lead. When he leapt into the sand on his final attempt, he thought he had done it. But when he saw the measurement, it was not what he was expecting to see. As it turns out, officials had ruled that his left hand grazed the sand before his feet touched the sand, giving him a 25-6 ¼ jump and costing him a medal. He ended up in a controversial fourth place.

Jeff Henderson captured the United States' first gold medal in the long jump since 2004.

Questions For Thought:
1. Jarrion's feats have been matched the great Jesse Owens accomplished over 80 years ago. What sports hero can you learn from?
2. Jarrion recognizes the importance of a great education. How much emphasis do you put on learning?
3. How do you balance academics and athletics?

Chaunté Lowe

Flying High

When Chaunté Lowe was in sixth grade, she returned home from a track meet to find her family had lost their house. Her sisters had been sent to live with their father, who, trapped by drug addictions, spent most of his adult life in prison. Her mother struggled from her own addiction problems, and after they lost the house, Chaunté slept with her mother in rundown hotels and backs of cars. Chaunté was sent to live with an aunt, and eventually decided to live with her grandmother.

Embracing the sport of track and field was logical coming from a poverty standpoint. All it required was shorts and shoes. She was a sprinter, hurdler, and triple jumper, and made the national honor roll. She went on to Georgia Tech, where she became the school's first-ever female Olympian when she qualified for the 2004 Olympic Games in Athens as a sophomore.

In 2008, Chaunté and her husband, Mario, purchased their first home. With a new baby, she soon found out it's not easy for a new mother to remain competitive, and was unable to earn money as an athlete. The economic crash of 2008 hit the couple hard. They purchased a rental property one day, and Mario lost his job the next. Both of their homes went into foreclosure. She and Mario moved into a tiny, one-bedroom apartment. Chaunté gave birth again, and this daughter had Asperger's syndrome.

Chaunté's Olympic performance had perhaps not yet matched her expectations in part because she was nursing children or recovering from childbirth. In 2004, she finished 13th in qualifying. In 2008, she placed sixth at the Beijing Olympics. In 2012, she went to the London Games as a favorite to medal, and again finished sixth. Chaunté had a tough 2015. She moved her training home base from Atlanta to Florida to obtain care for her special needs daughter.

Entering the Rio Games, Chaunté had cleared 6-7 at the U.S. Olympic Trials, the year's best mark in the world. Chaunté and three other jumpers were the only ones to make it to the final round of jumps. Chaunté was the final jumper. If she had cleared it, she would have won the gold. But she failed to do so and once again, she missed the podium by just one spot, finishing 4th.

Despite never earning an Olympic gold medal, Chaunté Lowe has been a great inspiration in the sport of track and field.

Questions For Thought:

1. Chaunté has made her family a priority. What are the important things in your life?
2. Chaunté has made four Olympic teams. What attributes does she possess that have led her to success?
3. Chaunté enjoys her high jumping and entertaining the crowd. She has fun with her sport. Do you have fun with your sport?

Maggie Malone

NCAA & Olympic Trials Champion

Things just kept getting better and better for javelin thrower Maggie Malone. She started by breaking the Texas A&M school record of 198 feet in March of 2016. A couple months later, she broke the collegiate record as she won the NCAA javelin title with a throw of 204 feet. This put her at No. 4 on the American all-time list and she also has the No. 1, No. 4, No. 7 and No. 8 all-time collegiate performances.

Malone started her career as a Nebraska Cornhusker, where she won the Big Ten javelin title as a sophomore, earned All-America status twice at the NCAA meet, and competed well in the heptathlon. She then learned her coach, Kris Grimes, was leaving for a coaching position at Texas A&M. Coincidentally, Maggie's family had recently moved to Bryan-College Station, Texas. When she told her parents she wanted to follow Coach Grimes, she didn't even know where A&M was—in the same town as her family. She stayed at Nebraska for another year but made the move to Texas A&M for her final two years of school and competition.

After some adjustments, an increase in strength, and improvement in technique, Malone became the first female javelin thrower to win the NCAA and Olympic Trials in the same year. She won the Trials with a throw of 199-7. In Rio, however, she could only manage a throw of 185-3 in the qualifying round, placing 25th.

Questions For Thought:

1. Maggie used an increase in strength for improvement. What else can you improve in to help performances?
2. Maggie became the first female thrower to win both NCAA and Olympic Trials titles in the same year. Competing in the collegiate season and the Olympics makes for a long season. How do you stay motivated over a long season?
3. Maggie was willing to move to continue to receive good coaching. How have coaches made a difference in your life?

Brenda Martinez

Against the Odds

The odds were against Brenda Martinez. She grew up in a working-class family with Mexican immigrant parents in Rancho Cucamonga, California. Her parents worked two jobs and her mom sold tamales to help pay for track meet fees.

She was an NCAA 1500 runner-up for UC Riverside, where she became her family's first college graduate. After graduating in 2010, Martinez drifted and struggled with running and was turned down by high-profile, elite training groups after graduation. There were times when she and her husband/coach, Carlos Handler, were so financially strapped that they had to choose between paying the rent and eating. Still she kept on training.

She got her break when she contacted one of the most successful coaches in the sport, the retired Dr. Joe Vigil. It was Martinez's blue collar background and work ethic that brought Vigil out of retirement to write her workouts. The duo was anything but fancy—no underwater treadmills, fancy facilities, or doctors. Martinez and Handler even had to climb over fences at high school tracks to train at night and were kicked off multiple tracks in one day. But despite the odds, Martinez became the first U.S. woman to win a bronze medal in the 800 at the 2013 World Championships in Moscow.

Her road to Rio, however, was quite the trip. At the 2016 Trials, after easily advancing to the 800 meter final, Martinez rounded the final curve pulling within a stride or two from the leader and edging to take the lead, and possibly headed to victory and a sub-1:58. But she was accidentally tripped, was knocked into lane 3, and lost her momentum and ultimately her shot at the 800 Olympic team.

The adversity in her life taught her to learn and move on. Hoping to bounce back from the 800 meter nightmare, Brenda tried to steer clear of disaster in the 1500 meter final. She did stumble over feet several times throughout the race and was in sixth place heading into the final lap. But in the final 20 meters, she was stride for stride with Amanda Eccleston, and they both dove across the finish line for a chance at the third and final spot on the Olympic team. Brenda Martinez had made the team.

Despite the barriers she broke up to this point in her life, Martinez could not advance out of the semifinals in the 1500 in Rio. With 300 meters to go, it appeared Martinez just couldn't find another gear and fell to 12th, finishing in 4:10.41.

Questions For Thought:

1. Brenda takes great pride in her work ethic. Rate your work ethic on a scale of 1-10.
2. How would you describe your approach to training?
3. Adversity in life teaches lessons, what lessons has it taught you?

Tatyana McFadden

Paralympic Phenomenon

Tatyana McFadden was born in Russia and spent the first six years of her life in an orphanage. Tatyana was born with spina bifida, a hole in her spine, which left her paralyzed from the waist down. Growing up in the orphanage, she didn't have a wheelchair, so she learned to crawl and walk around on her arms in order to keep up with the other children. Tatyana was adopted by the Commissioner of Disabilities for the U.S. Department of Health, Deborah McFadden, who brought her to the U.S. to give her a wheelchair and a new life.

The upper body strength Tatyana began to develop as an orphan in Russia soon turned her into one of the world's greatest Paralympic athletes. In the U.S., Tatyana tried a variety of sports using her wheelchair, including basketball, swimming, ice hockey, and scuba diving. It was wheelchair racing that she found both joy and success. In high school, Tatyana was not allowed to compete alongside able-bodied runners, competing in a separate race usually alone, until her and her family won a lawsuit against the school system. The lawsuit led to a state law and then a national mandate guaranteeing all students with disabilities the right to participate in sports.

At the age of 15, she became the youngest member of Team USA at the 2004 Paralympics in Athens, and brought home a silver medal in the 100 meters and a bronze in the 200. Tatyana went on to compete on the wheelchair basketball and wheelchair track teams at the University of Illinois. At the 2008 Paralympics in Beijing, she earned four more medals. In London, in 2012, she added another four medals, three of which were gold. She holds the world record in the 100, 400, 800, 1,500 and 5,000 meters. One silver medal also came from the winter Paralympics, where Tatyanna competed in cross-country skiing in Sochi in 2014.

Tatyanna was poised to make history at the Rio Paralympics, as she became the first to compete in seven events in wheelchair racing and had a shot to win seven gold medals. Tatyana won the 400, 800, 1500 and 5000, but fell short of her seven golds by earning silver in the 100 and the marathon. She and the U.S. were disqualified from the 4x400 relay. She has a total of 17 career Paralympic medals.

When Tatyana McFadden was brought to the U.S., doctors told her mother she had little chance of being active or even surviving, but she surpassed all odds and became one of the world's top Paralympic athletes.

Questions For Thought:

1. Tatyanna's adopted mother gave her a new life. Who do you have to thank for your success?
2. Tatyanna used her strength in her upper body to her advantage in wheelchair racing. What are your strengths?
3. As a disabled athlete, Tatyanna could have given up, but she fought for her right to participate in sports. What are you willing to fight for?

Sydney McLaughlin

Hurdling High Schooler

Of the more than 100 athletes on the U.S. track-and-field delegation in Rio, 84 were first-time Olympians, according to USA Track & Field. Sydney McLaughlin was the youngest of these athletes to qualify for the US Olympic track and field team since Carol Lewis—Carl Lewis's sister—in 1980, the year the United States boycotted the Moscow Games, at the age of 16. Sydney turned 17 a week before the Games and opted to skip the opening ceremonies to celebrate her birthday.

Until she finished third at the Olympic Trials, she was focused on the cheeseburger she would eat after the race. But her plans changed significantly, as she was on her way to Rio. As a rising senior at Union Catholic Regional High School in Scotch Plains, New Jersey, McLaughlin's Trials time was the sixth-fastest in the world for 2016 in the 400 meter hurdles. That time of 54.15 was also a world junior record.

Earlier in the season, Sydney was halted during the first weeks of indoor track practice due to mononucleosis. Then, in April, her mother suffered a heart attack. Sydney and her mother recovered, and Sydney went on to smash records. McLaughlin set a national junior record in the indoor 400 meters, and went undefeated in the hurdles against high school competition. In June 2016, McLaughlin was chosen as the Gatorade Girls National High School Track and Field Athlete of the Year. Olympian Allyson Felix presented the award to Sydney by surprising her after a track workout.

In Rio, a rain storm left the track soaked, and her race was the first one after a short weather delay. She was also battling a cold that zapped her energy. McLaughlin was not one of the three automatic qualifiers in her heat, running 56.32 to finish fifth in the first of six heats. When only two runners topped her time, she moved onto the next round.

Her Rio run came to an end in the semi-finals but as the youngest athlete to compete for U.S. track and field, she returned to high school for her senior year. She will begin looking at colleges, and turning professional will be an option, working towards another shot at the Olympics in four years.

Questions for Thought:
1. Sydney overcame mono to have a record-breaking season. What mental skills can you use when you are sick or injured?
2. How do you balance activities in your life?
3. Once you achieve success, do you continue to work just as hard as you did before?

Hassan Mead

His Time Will Come

Hassan Mead has faced struggles his entire life. Hassan grew up on a small family farm in war-torn Somalia, near the border of Ethiopia. His job as a young boy was to keep the goats, sheep, cows and other wild animals away from the crops on his family's farm. His father emigrated to America in 1996 and four years later Hassan, then 11, followed with his mother and younger sister.

Hassan struggled with the cold temperatures as he had rarely experienced temperatures below 50 degrees. He went to California to stay with his uncle where he went to school for the first time. Hassan took up running and moved to the state of Washington finishing 10th in the state cross country met. His senior year, he reunited with his family in Minnesota and won the Class 2A cross-country state title. Mead was a six-time All-American in cross country and he won seven Big Ten titles in track for the University of Minnesota.

After 13 years of training, Hassan felt confident he could make the U.S. Olympic team at 10,000 meters. It was hot and he began to struggle; he went from the lead group to flat on his back in a matter of minutes. Though his spirits were low after dropping out of the 10K, his teammates and coach rallied around him and convinced him he still had a chance of making the team in the 5K. Five days later, Mead had regained enough strength and confidence to come back in the 5000 and compete for a spot on the Olympic team. Finishing with the best sprint of his life, he made his first Olympic team.

In Rio, Hassan was in position to finish in the top five of his first-round race to automatically advance to the final with about 250 meters to go when he was tripped and fell to the track. He got up to finish 13th, but it wasn't good enough to advance. Hassan filed a protest in hopes to be advanced to the final, but the protest was initially denied. Later, the IAAF announced that Hassan would be moved into the final after examining new video evidence.

Hassan ran in third place early in the 5000 final. Around 800 meters, he dropped toward the back of the pack and waited until the 3K mark to make a move to fifth. Though his goal was to finish in the top 10 at his first Olympic Games, he fell back on the final lap and ended up finishing 11th in 13:09.81.

Questions For Thought:

1. Hassan's friends encouraged him to come back and make the Olympic team at 5000 meters. How do you make a difference in others' lives?
2. Hassan got up after his fall in the Olympic 5000 and finished the race so that he could protest for a chance to make the final. Have you ever fallen and come back stronger than ever?
3. Hassan's goal was to finish in the top 10 at the Olympics but he finished 11th. When you don't achieve your goal, do you keep trying?

Aries Merritt

Transplant to Success

Aries Merritt was on top of the world in 2012, with an Olympic gold medal and a world record of 12.80 seconds in the 110-meter hurdles, and he recorded the most sub-13-second races in a single season by any athlete. In 2015, Aries Merritt was on top of an operating table.

His kidneys began to fail in 2013 and he was told he might never run again as a result of collapsing focal segmental glomerulosclerosis, a progressive form of kidney disease. The diagnosis turned Aries into a depressed, angry, and mean person. He battled this illness with kidneys functioning at only 10 percent to win a bronze medal at the 2015 world championships in a season-best time, just a week before undergoing his kidney transplant thanks in part to his sister, who served as his kidney donor.

Doctors told Aries he had to wait eight weeks to return to training. He was able to get going in seven, then needed to wait several more weeks when his new kidney needed a second surgery in October. After a single day of training, he had developed a hematoma. Aries didn't lift weights for two months after surgery. He takes medication for his kidney every 12 hours, but the drugs are either neutral or could slightly weaken muscles.

Though maybe not as strong, Aries felt as though he was in better shape than ever going into the 2016 Olympic Trials. Approximately 10 months post-surgery, he had also been recovering from a torn groin in recent weeks. Aries launched from the starting blocks in the 110-meter hurdles final, his trail leg grazing the transplant scar across his abdomen 10 times as he cleared each hurdle. An agonizing wait for the time to show up on the scoreboard showed that Aries missed the 2016 Olympic team by the cruelest of margins: one one-hundredth of one second. Aries thought he finished second or third and asked for the photo finish to be review, but the result stood.

Despite barely missing his second Olympic team, Aries Merritt still holds the world record in the 110-meter hurdles. But more importantly, he has set the standard for courageous effort.

Questions For Thought:

1. With his kidneys only operating at 10%, Aries won a silver medal in the 2015 World Championships. What is your reaction to this performance?
2. Aries couldn't wait to resume training. How anxious are you to improve your game?
3. What does courage mean to you?

Shaunae Miller

Accidental Dive

Bahamas sprinter Shaunae Miller may have won the Olympic 400 meter gold on accident. How does that happen?

At the 2011 World Youth Championships, Shaunae became the first athlete from the Bahamas to win the 400 meters. Shaunae ran for the University of Georgia and competed in the 2012 Olympic Games, though she did not finish her heat. Shaunae was in her prime in 2016. She won the 400 meters at the Prefontaine Classic, competing against the best in the world. She entered the 2016 Olympics as one of the favorites in the 400 meters.

Shaunae had been leading for the first half of the Olympic 400-meter final, drawing lane seven and getting out fast. Her race plan was to take full control of the race. Shaunae executed her race plan perfectly, running the final curve strong to gain a lead entering the homestretch. Shaunae and Allyson Felix of the United States came neck and neck, and it looked like Felix would take the gold; a record fifth win at the Games. But Shaunae lost feelings in her legs and lunged forward in a final attempt to win, diving across the line and landing on her face .07 seconds before Felix could get to the line. Both athletes, Shaunae praying on her back, Felix sprawled on the track, waited 15 seconds before the results appeared on the scoreboard. Shaunae took the gold with a personal best time of 49.44, and Felix was second in 49.51.

Controversy on social media surrounded the dive, debating whether the move was fair, ethical, or even legal. But the move is in fact legal, and it is common in the sport of track and field. Rule 164 of the IAAF Competition Rulebook states: *"The athletes shall be placed in the order in which any part of their bodies (i.e. torso, as distinguished from the head, neck, arms, legs, hands or feet) reaches the vertical plane of the near edge of the finish line as defined above."*

Shaunae Miller stated after the race that she didn't mean to dive. All she remembers is that her legs became heavy and she started to lose feeling in them, so she did whatever she could to get across the line. Maybe it was an accident, but it worked.

Questions For Thought:

1. Shaunae put herself in position to win. How do you put yourself in a winning position?
2. Shaunae carried out her race plan. Do you plan your strategy?
3. When you start feeling fatigue, what mental strategies do you use?

Heather Miller-Koch

Multi-Tasker

At one point in her life, Heather Miller-Koch had her life planned out. She was going to milk cows in the morning, go to work as a nurse, and come back to milk cows in the evening. At some point, however, the Olympics entered her life plan.

After her career as two-sport athlete at St. Cloud State, where she was a 10-time All American, she decided to set her sights on the Olympic heptathlon. Residing in Mendota Heights, Minnesota, Heather was balancing work as an orthopedic surgery nurse at United Hospital in St. Paul with training. With little time off her feet and being unable to hydrate enough due to being stuck in surgery for hours at a time, the balance meant sacrifice. Eventually, she began working only part time to take her goals seriously and stay healthy. She finished fourth at both the 2014 and 2015 USA Outdoor Championships. She was 14 points shy of earning a World Championship berth in 2015, but failed to crack the top three for a third straight year.

In November of 2015, Heather took a year long sabbatical from nursing, and moved to train full time at the Olympic Training Center with her husband/coach in California. Her second place performance at the U.S. Olympic Trials was the 10th highest American score all time.

Day one in Rio saw Heather overcome physical and mental difficulty with a different type of heptathlon schedule athletes are normally used to, having morning and night sessions rather than 30 minutes between each event. Going into the final event of the heptathlon, Heather was confident that she was ready to run a fast 800—and she was. She ran a personal best of 2:06.82, the sixth fastest time ever run in an Olympic heptathlon 800, winning the seventh and final event of all 29 athletes in the competition. Her time boosted her four spots to 18th place with 6,213 points.

Questions For Thought:

1. Heather struggled to balance work and training. What things in your life do you have to successfully balance?
2. Are you confident that you have properly prepared for a key event?
3. How can you successfully visualize yourself obtaining your goals?

Alysia Montaño

Heartbreak Hero

As the rest of the 800-meter field ran away from her at the 2016 US Olympic Trials, Alysia Montaño's dreams of a well-earned Olympic medal did too.

The incident occurred during the 800 meter final, and Alysia was sitting in position to make her move off the curve when she clipped the heels of Brenda Martinez. Martinez stumbled into lane three and Alysia ended up on the track. When she fell, all she could think was, "get up, get up."

Alysia did get up. She jogged a bit, then stopped, fell to her knees, and began to wail as she kicked her foot to the ground in disgust. She got up again and ran to the finish line, then collapsed to her knees, put her head on the ground, looked skyward, clutched her right hand to her heart and let out a primal wail.

But it was too late; they were too far gone. Kate Grace went on to win, with Ajeé Wilson and an unexpected Chrishuna Williams making the team as well. The race wasn't supposed to go like that, but then again, Alysia's entire professional running career didn't go the way she had planned.

It was an agonizing end to a discouraging season, as she had been coping with the fallout of a Russian doping scandal. She is a six-time U.S. champion and placed fifth in the 800 meters at the 2012 Olympics. If the Russian athletes who have since tested positive for performance-enhancing drugs were to be stripped of their medals, Alysia would have a silver medal from the 2010 world indoor championships and three bronze medals from the 2012 Olympics and the 2011 and 2013 outdoor world championships. After the London heartbreak, Alysia considered quitting. Instead, she gave birth to daughter Linnéa, competing in the 2014 USA Outdoor Track and Field Championships while eight months pregnant.

Alysia Montaño has poured her heart and soul into a long and successful career. Her unfortunate accident in the 2016 Trials was heartbreaking considering all the effort put forth to be a world-class athlete.

Questions For Thought:

1. When your hopes are crushed, do you stay down?
2. Alysia finished the race even when there was no chance to make the team. Do you finish what you start?
3. Alysia has been denied Olympic glory due to competitors using performance-enhancing drugs. Are you a strong advocate of competing clean?

Sandi Morris

Flying Squirrel

Sandi Morris is nicknamed the "Flying Squirrel" because she leaps from high places on the track in pole vault, and her personality has her jumping from hobby to hobby and always looking for an adventure.

Sandi won two South Carolina high school state championships and earned a scholarship to vault at the University of North Carolina. In her first year, Sandi was the only freshman to advance to indoor nationals and clear 14 feet. Her sophomore year, she struggled with the mental aspect of the sport and in the classroom. Though she was on the brink of making it to the 2012 Olympic Trials, she couldn't quite hit the qualifying standard.

Sandi transferred to Arkansas, where some of the best pole vaulters in NCAA history were. In 2015, Sandi broke the collegiate record at the second meet of the indoor season and jumped the current NCAA outdoor record at 15-5 ¾. She became a Bowerman semifinalist, a four-time All-American, a Nike athlete, and jumped for Team USA at the IAAF World Championships.

In May of 2016, Sandi snapped a pole and broke her left wrist at a meet in the Czech Republic. Seven weeks out from the Olympic Trials, she was able to run and train but couldn't vault for four weeks. At the Trials, she overcame the pain and finished second behind 2012 Olympic gold medalist Jenn Suhr.

On July 24, 2016, just days after the Trials, Sandi broke the outdoor American record at the American Track League meet in Houston. With a jump of 16-2, she scraped by Indoor World and American record-holder Jenn Suhr's previous outdoor record of 16-1 ½, set in 2006.

In Rio, Sandi missed her first attempts of 15-4 and 15-7, but cleared the heights on her second try, before missing three attempts at 16-0 ¾. Neither Morris nor Greece's Ekaterini Stefanidi cleared 16-0 ¾, but Stefanidi had one fewer miss than Sandi on the night, leaving Sandi with the silver medal.

With a silver medal on her plate and aiming for gold in four years, Sandi Morris went on to compete at the Brussels Diamond League meet after Rio. There, she shattered her outdoor American record when she cleared a height of 16-5 to win, making her only the second woman ever to clear 16-5 outdoors.

Questions For Thought:

1. Sandi Morris transferred to be surrounded by good vaulters. How do the people around you make you better?
2. How do you maintain your physical and mental condition when you are injured?
3. The pole vault requires a great amount of focus. How important is the skill of being able to focus well? How do you develop your ability to focus?

Dalilah Muhammad

Barrier Champion

Dalilah Muhammad has been overcoming hurdles, literally and metaphorically, since she started running when she was seven years old. It wasn't until she was in high school that she decided she would focus on hurdling over literal obstacles. But she didn't see the metaphorical hurdles that were to come.

Delilah won the 400-meter hurdles 2007 IAAF World Youth title while in high school and went to the University of Southern California with a high school personal best of 57.09. In 2012, Dalilah came up short in the Trials, eliminated early in the qualifying heats. After somewhat of a stagnant college career, Dalilah had a breakthrough 2013 season. She won the USATF championship with a personal best of 53.83 and went on to earn a silver medal at the IAAF World Championships in Moscow.

In 2014, she failed to live up to her potential, running in just two 400-meter hurdle races that year, failing to finish under 58 seconds in either race—a mark she regularly surpassed in high school. 2015 didn't prove to be much better, as she injured her quad and could not keep her fitness level up to par through cross training. It was at this point she realized she needed a change in coaching and left to join coach Lawrence Johnson in February 2016. Johnson's training group includes fellow Olympian hurdlers Kristi Castlin and Brianna Rollins.

The change paid off, as Dalilah ran her season's best time, 54.15, to outpace her competitors by more than a second at the 2016 Olympic Trials. She didn't know if she could go any faster than that or if her body was even capable of doing so—but she did. In the finals, she set a new U.S. Olympic Trials record, the fastest time in the world in 2016, the fifth-fastest time in American history, and the 13th-fastest time in world history with a 52.88.

Though not as fast but just as, if not more, impressive, Delilah Muhammad made history in Rio. She took a commanding lead early, finding herself all alone in the final 100 meters, cruising to the finish in 53.13 seconds. It was the first time an American woman had ever won a gold medal in the event.

Questions For Thought:

1. Dalilah made history in Rio. What can you learn from the history of those who came before you?
2. Sometimes a change is for the good. What changes have you made that have worked out for the good?
3. Despite ups and downs, how can you be more consistent?

Clayton Murphy

Olympic Surprise

Clayton Murphy grew up on a farm in the Midwest, showing and selling pigs at agricultural fairs before focusing on sports. In a town of about 890 people with a high school graduating class of 60, Clayton was one of six people on Tri-Village High School's cross country team. He was a strong but unheralded high school runner, running 1:54 for 800 meters as a junior. He raced as an unknown for most of his career.

Clayton won an Ohio Division IV state title his senior year in high school in the 1600, setting a state record of 4:11.72. He went on to Division 1 Akron University where he won two NCAA titles in the 800 indoor and the 1500 outdoor. Clayton finished fourth as a 20-year-old at the USATF Outdoor Championships and went on to win the 800 at the 2015 Pan-Am Games in Toronto and was second at the North American Central American and Caribbean Championships. When U.S. 800-meter champion Nick Symmonds dropped out of the IAAF World Championships, Clayton was called to represent Team USA in Beijing. Murphy shocked everyone when he finished as the top U.S. finisher and making it to the semifinals, topping Cas Loxsom and Erik Sowinski. Clayton was no longer an unknown. He was one of the best runners in the country.

He gave up his final season of eligibility to sign with Nike as a professional athlete. Earlier in the year, Clayton and his coach, Lee LaBadie, had decided to concentrate on the 1500, but when he missed the Olympic qualifying standard by a hundredth of a second twice, they turned to the 800.

Clayton won the 800 meters at the Olympic Trials in 1:44.76, earning a PR and a spot on the Olympic team in Rio. His late kick allowed him to pass fellow Olympian Boris Berian for the win. When he got to Rio, his biggest goal was to have fun and make the final. But after running a near-flawless race that allowed him to use his kick on the homestretch to overtake Pierre-Ambroise Bosse of France with about 250 meters to go, he did more than just make the final. With a personal best time of 1:42.93, Murphy finished third behind defending champion and world-record holder David Rudisha of Kenya (1:42.15) and Taoufik Makhloufi of Algeria (1:42.61). Clayton won the United State's first medal in the event since 1992, when Johnny Gray won a bronze medal at the Barcelona Games.

Questions For Thought:

1. Clayton was overshadowed by other Ohio prep standout athletes during high school, but continued to persist. Do you have persistence?
2. Clayton and his coach originally decided to focus on the 1500, but later switched to the 800. Have you ever made a last minute decision that turned out for the better?
3. The last U.S. Olympic medal in the 800 was from Johnny Gray in 1992. Gray was not afraid to step out of his comfort zone and push the pace, where as Clayton likes to sit and kick. How do you plan your strategy?

Keturah Orji

Tripling to History

Triple jumper Keturah Orji hadn't lost a competition since her first collegiate track meet as a freshman at the University of Georgia. Even then, she placed second. She was 8-0 through two collegiate outdoor seasons in the triple jump and won three NCAA titles after winning the 2015 outdoor title and sweeping the indoor and outdoor championships in 2016. She set the collegiate and American record of 47-8 in the triple jump at the 2016 NCAA outdoor track and field championships.

The U.S. Olympic Trials were no different, and it only took one jump for her to set herself apart from the competition, as she jumped 46-11 ¾. She would have qualified for the team with any of her six jumps, and five of the six would have kept her in first.

In Rio, Keturah struggled in the qualifying round and was the last competitor to qualify for the final. On her first jump in the final she went big, once again set an American record on her first jump, bumping her own record up to 48-3 ¼ and putting her in the early lead. She was eventually bumped to fourth place, where she would remain. She missed the bronze medal by just 1¼ inches. Though she fouled on her second and third jumps, her first was good enough to earn her three more jumps, however, she failed to better her first mark.

Keturah became the first American to advance to the triple jump finals in 20 years and the first female American to ever qualify for the final three jumps. Keturah Orji's future looks bright as she has produced the top three U.S. jumps ever.

Questions For Thought:

1. The triple jump has not been a strong suite for American women, but Keturah is changing that. What does it take to make change?
2. Keturah put her early struggles of the qualifying round behind her and jumped an American record on her first jump in the finals. Is getting off to a good start important to you?
3. How do you refocus when you make a mistake?

Brittney Reese

Committed to Service

Brittney Reese first attended Mississippi Gulf Coast Community College, then went on to the University of Mississippi, where she was the NCAA Outdoor Champion in the long jump in 2007 and 2008. She qualified for the 2008 Olympics by setting a new personal best of 22-9 ¾ at the Trials, but only managed to place fifth in the finals in Beijing.

Off the track, Reese is committed to giving back to youth and the community that has supported her throughout her athletic career. In 2011, she donated 100 turkeys for Thanksgiving and her time to various homeless and religious organizations in her community of Gulfport, Mississippi as her way of giving back to an area where there are few resources for those in need. Established in 2012, each year, Brittney gives a college scholarship to one male and one female high school senior in her hometown. She uses her platform to speak to youth and women's organizations about a healthy diet and exercise, hoping to help end childhood obesity. She is also an advocate against animal cruelty and volunteers with the American Society for the Prevention of Cruelty to Animals. It was for these endeavors that she was honored at the Shadow League Leadership Awards.

After winning her first Olympic gold medal in London in 2012, Brittney set out to do something no other woman had ever done—win two consecutive gold medals in the long jump. But in 2013, a torn hip labrum forced the three-time Olympian to undergo surgery. She rushed back from surgery but continued to struggle and contemplated retirement. Instead, she reached out to a sports psychologist who could help her work out the kinks off the track as she regained her physical form.

At age 29, Brittney was one of the oldest athletes in the Olympic long jump competition, along with American teammate Tianna Bartoletta, age 30. While separated by a year in age, less than an inch separated them in competition. Known as the "Long Jump Beast," Brittney was attempting to defend her Olympic title, but had trouble finding her groove in the finals. She fouled three of her first four attempts before finally turning in 23-3 and 23-5 ½ jumps. Brittney clapped her hands in frustration after the final jump, knowing it wasn't good enough to beat Bartoletta's jump. With that, Brittney Reese became just the second woman in American history to win multiple Olympic medals in the event behind Jackie Joyner-Kersee.

Questions For Thought:

1. Britney has often come down to her final jump with the pressure on and delivered. What does it take to deliver with the pressure on?
2. Britney gives backs to society. In what ways might you help better society?
3. Brittney practices the mental component of performances. How is your mental skill development program? How could you improve it?

Brianna Rollins

From Rags to Rio

Her high school coach told her she could do it. She just had to believe it.

Brianna Rollins grew up with six younger brothers and her mother had a hard time landing jobs to earn money for her family. Sometimes they had no running water, no electricity, no food. Eventually, they had to move in with Brianna's grandparents. Nothing came easy for the Rollins', but with the help of her high school coach, friends, and relatives, Brianna slowly came to realize her potential as a person and an athlete.

Brianna was a scrawny ninth grader who had never competed in sports, so when she showed up in Miami Northwestern High track coach Carmen Jackson's office asking to join the track team, she had her doubts. She turned out to be a phenomenal athlete in high school, but struggled academically and lacked focus, easily distracted by boyfriends. Jackson set her straight. She helped her get her priorities in order and she signed with Clemson her senior year.

At Clemson, she grew homesick and lazy. She despised the cold, and would quit workouts when she felt even a little pain. Once again, Jackson put her in her place—she told Brianna not to invite her to the pity party. And by her junior year in college, Brianna began to take things seriously on the track and in the classroom.

The 100-meter hurdles is one of the most competitive events in U.S. track and field. But after winning numerous conference titles, an NCAA indoor title as a sophomore at Clemson, and the NCAA outdoor title her senior year followed by breaking Gail Devers' 13-year-old U.S. record, Brianna made herself known in the hurdle world.

At the 2016 Olympic Trials at Hayward Field, nine women were ranked in the top 10 in the world in the 100-meter hurdles. But just three would make the Olympic team. Brianna was one of them as she won the gold.

In Rio, the US completed a first-ever 1-2-3 sweep in the event, with Brianna on top as the Olympic champion. Jackson had once told her she 'could break the world record, she could win the Olympics.' As Brianna Rollins crossed the finish line, her high school coach yelled "From rags to Rio!"

Questions For Thought:

1. Brianna originally struggled academically due to lack of focus, but had a support system to get her on track. Who is your support system and how do they get you on track?
2. At one time Brianna considered herself lazy. What are the odds of success if you are not willing to work for it?
3. Is it possible to take a sport seriously and still have fun?

Shannon Rowbury

Dressing for the Occasion

If Shannon Rowbury's 1500-meter American record and long list of accolades doesn't catch your attention, her pink lipstick will. Her hot pink lipstick isn't just for looks. It is a way to pay homage to her late grandmother—a tough, positive, and inspirational woman. When you wear hot pink lipstick, you better bring your A game. When you get dressed up for important events—as women in her grandmother's generation often did—it better be a special occasion. And it often is when Shannon steps on the track.

Before she was a three-time Olympian, Shannon was a star at Duke University, where she became a six-time NCAA All-American, a two-time NCAA runner up, and the 2007 NCAA national champion in the mile.

In the 2008 Beijing Olympics, Shannon was 7th in the 1500 meter. In the 2012 Olympic 1500, she bettered that by just one place. However, since then, six women in that field have either been banned or are facing allegations of performance enhancing drug use. These allegations have left Shannon feeling as though she was robbed of what would have been the silver medal. An advocate for clean sports, she is also a co-founder of the non-profit organization Imagining More, whose mission is to serve as an instrument for young women who wish to develop in arts and sports as well as to create awareness about the uniqueness of being a female athlete.

Four years later, the International Olympic Committee has yet to reverse the 2012 results or reallocate any of the medals. In Rio, Shannon barely missed a second chance at an Olympic medal, finishing fourth behind Kenya's Faith Kipyegon, Ethiopia's Genzebe Dibaba and fellow American Jenny Simpson.

Shannon Rowbury left the 2016 Olympics devastated with the lack of a medal. However, she quickly turned disappointment into success by setting an American record in the 5000, running 14:38.92 in a Brussels Diamond League meet.

Questions For Thought:

1. How do you get "dressed up" for special performances?
2. What stand are you taking on the use of performance-enhancing drugs?
3. Shannon is helping young women develop outside of sports. What are you doing to get better outside of sports?

David Rudisha

King of the 800

David Rudisha is the "King" in his homeland as a member of the Maasai tribe in Narok County, southwest Kenya. He is the son of a silver medalist in the at the 1968 Olympics in Mexico City, a father of two daughters, and a police officer through Kenya's national service program. He is also a two-time Olympic gold medalist and the world record holder at 800 meters.

David's career has been long lived. He won his first international medal at the 2006 World Junior Championships in Beijing. He was named the male Athlete of the Year in 2010 by the International Association of Athletics Federations (IAAF), intersecting a five-year streak of Usain Bolt winning the award. After winning the 800-meter title in London in 2012, David suffered through three years of frustration and only occasional elation following keyhole surgery on a serious knee injury, which caused him to miss the World Championships in 2013.

In 2016, he was ready to show the world that David Rudisha was back. But two hours before race time, rain began to fall in Rio and David was nervous. Rain hadn't been friendly to him in the past—it led to under-performances at the World Championships in Berlin in 2009, Milan in 2010, Zurich in 2012, The Commonwealth Games in Glasgow, and in the Stockholm Diamond League earlier in 2016. The rain is partly a mental thing, but David thinks it makes him feel stiff.

Despite the rain, David continued to relax, and the skies eventually cleared to allow him to run his race with confidence. Kenyan compatriot Alfred Kipketer charged to try to take the early lead with a blistering pace, clashing elbows with David and causing him to fall back five or six meters. He remained composed and knew Kipketer's pace was unattainable. With 250 meters remaining, David Rudisha established a decisive lead in a few strides before storming away to win in 1:42.16 – his fastest time since winning the London 2012 gold.

Questions For Thought:

1. David Rudisha has set the bar high with a world record. He likes to run from the front of the pack and is an aggressive but smart runner. Are you a smart competitor?
2. Do you develop your skills under different environmental conditions?
3. How can you mentally train for distractions that may occur?

Galen Rupp

Movin' On Up

After a fifth place finish in both the 5000 and 10,000 meter at the 2015 world championships in Beijing, both Galen Rupp and his coach, Alberto Salazar, knew it was time for a change. Although he was one of only six Americans to have run under 13:00 for 5000 meters and won the first American medal in 10,000 since Billy Mills' gold in 1964, Salazar introduced Galen to the idea of the marathon. From there, they altered his strength-training regimen to reduce upper body bulk and to give him a more fluid, flexible, yet still powerful stride fit for the marathon.

Heading into his first marathon ever, Galen was running 145 miles a week, with 30 of those miles being on an underwater treadmill. He delivered a dominant performance of 2:11:12 to win the 2016 U.S. Olympic Trials in February. In July, Galen also qualified for the Olympic 10,000 meter in a race that saw many of the nation's top runners fade or drop out due to 82-degree temperatures. It was his eighth consecutive U.S. title at the distance, and the performance qualified him for his third straight Olympic berth in the 10,000. Though his original plans were to focus on the 10K and the marathon in Rio, Galen surprised many by hoping to defend his 5000 Trials title from four years prior and become the first American to win a 5K, 10K, and marathon national title in the same year. However, his marathon training proved to take too much away from his leg speed and he finished ninth in the 5K in 13:41.09.

Galen went into the Games hoping to complete an "Olympic double," earning a medal in both the 10,000 and the marathon. In the 10K, he got tangled up with his training partner, Mo Farah, around lap 16, and blood dripped from his leg after he was spiked. Ultimately, Galen couldn't come away with a medal like he did in 2012, finishing fifth in 27:08.92. Galen had to move on from the disappointment and focus on the marathon, which was a week away. Many had tried their hands at both the marathon and 10,000, the most demanding distance races at the Summer Games, but nearly all had failed in their attempt.

Galen captured bronze in a time of 2:10:05 in a steady rain in Rio, becoming the first American to medal in the event since 2004 and just the third since 1924. Galen Rupp has led a resurgence of U.S. distance runners who are achieving success at the world level. The U.S. won six medals in Rio in races of at least 1500 meters.

Questions For Thought:

1. Galen's coach decided he should make a training and racing change. What changes have you made that have turned out well?
2. Galen was running 145 miles a week to train for the marathon. When you have a big work load, how do you manage your time?
3. When others have failed at something in the past, what thoughts do you have? How can you overcome negative thoughts to help you achieve your goal?

Greg Rutherford

Risk Taker

Britain's Greg Rutherford was risking more than most athletes when he stepped on the runway at the Rio Games. Athletes spend months and even years to reach the peak point in their fitness in order to reap the benefits for just a short time. But Greg may bear the brunt of it for the rest of his life. He suffered whiplash from a fall during the long jump competition at the Birmingham Diamond League meet in June of 2016. The injury caused a hearing loss condition called cochlear hydrops, and there is a one in four chance that his hearing will be a lifelong affliction.

Greg actually lived a risky lifestyle up until the age of 17, when he had a revelation while "car surfing" with his brother and friend. He had frequently engaged in the activity, which entails lying lie face down and wrapping your arms around the roof of a car while somebody drives around 50 miles per hour down a country lane. It was on top of a car where he realized that if he falls off and dies, he'd never make it in any sport. He had tried many sports at the time, including football, rugby, cricket, and badminton—but he hated to lose and didn't want to be half-decent at those. When he found long jump, he discovered true euphoria.

He has suffered several other injuries throughout his long jumping career, including a ruptured hamstring, three operations on his knee and ankle, a left adductor tear, multiple hernias requiring surgeries, a problematic bone spur in his ankle, and appendicitis. Greg admitted had it not been an Olympic year, he probably would have taken some time off to address his hearing condition.

However, Greg was looking to defend his title after he won gold for Great Britain in 2012 with a jump of 27-3. He went to Rio as only the fifth Britain to hold the Olympic, World, Commonwealth and European athletic titles in the same cycle. But his longest jump — a sixth and final attempt of 27-2 ½ — moved him up from fourth to third. Jeff Henderson of the United States then went even further with his final jump, jumping 27-6 to take gold.

Questions For Thought:

1. Greg is a risk taker. How can that be a good thing in your sport? How can it be a bad thing?
2. Greg suffered through numerous injuries and competed at the Olympics with hearing loss due to a whiplash injury. How do you know when to fight through the pain or when you should take time to address the injury?
3. Greg may bear the burden of his long jumping injury for a lifetime. How far are you willing to go?

Raven Saunders

Support of Family and Friends

Shot putter Raven Saunders has a whole community behind her just waiting to send her on her way to her next chance at success. When she qualified for the U.S. Junior Nationals in 2014, nearly 100 people from Charleston, South Carolina donated more than $6,000 to send her to Eugene, Oregon. When she qualified for the 2016 Olympics as an Ole Miss sophomore, her village backed her up. Though the U.S. Olympic Committee covered Raven's expenses, more than 370 people donated $22,895 to send her family to Brazil.

Growing up just 20-25 minutes from the beach, many of the children in Raven's neighborhood had never even seen the ocean. Thanks to Raven's friends and family and track and field, she has already seen much of the world. Those same friends and family have always been her backbone. When her grandmother passed away in February 2016, Raven was on the verge of going back home to be with her mom and sister. Her grandmother was a devout member of the Emmanuel AME Church, the same church Raven was baptized at. The same church at which nine of its members were brutally murdered in June of 2015 and Raven dedicated her USATF Outdoor Senior Nationals performance to. But it was her family members who convinced her to continue to compete in her grandmother's honor.

The indoor and outdoor NCAA champion as a true freshman for Southern Illinois University, Raven also set the Missouri Valley Conference's indoor, outdoor and all-time records in the shot. In 2016, she won the outdoor shot put NCAA crown and set the all-time collegiate record in both the indoor and outdoor events. Her winning throw of 63-5 at the NCAA outdoor championships is the longest throw ever by a collegian. At the 2016 U.S. Olympic Trials, Raven fouled two of her first three throws in the final, but her second throw was enough to get into the finals. Raven then earned her spot on the Olympic team with a throw that catapulted her from fourth to second.

In an event that saw a fellow American make history, Raven Saunders held her own at the Olympics. With her mom, her aunt and her sister in the stands, she threw a career best of 63-6 for fifth place. Gold medalist Michelle Carter threw 67-8 ¼ on her final attempt to set a new American record and become the first American woman to medal in that event.

Questions For Thought:

1. Raven Saunders has much support of family and friends. How do your family and friends support you?
2. How do you appreciate their support?
3. Raven counts her many blessings on her path to success. How do you count your blessings?

Jenny Simpson

Third Time's the Charm

As the saying goes, "the third time's the charm" for Jenny Simpson.

The former University of Colorado runner qualified for three Olympic teams before finally securing a medal and a spot on the podium. As a Buffalo, Jenny won the 2006 NCAA Outdoor steeplechase. She then went on to qualify for the 2008 Olympics in Beijing in the 3000-meter steeplechase, the first time the event was contested in Olympic history. She finished 9th, but set an American record of 9:22.26.

After focusing on the steeplechase for her first three years at the University of Colorado and competing in one Olympic Games, Jenny shifted her focus to running events ranging from 1500 to 5000 meters.

She won gold in the 1500 at the Daegu 2011 World Championships and in 2012, Jenny advanced to the semi-final round of the 1500 meter in the London Games. She went on to earn a silver in the 1500 at the Moscow World Championships in 2013.

In her 2016 quest to earn that elusive Olympic medal, Jenny secured her spot in a third Olympics by winning the 1500 meter at the Olympic Trials with a time of 4:04.74. In Rio, the race started out slow and tactical, but when Ethiopia's Genzebe Dibaba exploded to the lead after 700 meters, Jenny focused on the medal spots ahead of her. Jenny entered the 1500 final with a focus to "position the first 2 laps and the second two laps become a predator." Jenny ran her final 800 meters in 1:58.9, faster than she has ever run an 800-meter race in her life. Always a threat in the homestretch, she ran a well-timed race, moving from 6th at the bell to move up. With 30 meters to go, Jenny Simpson caught Netherlands' Sifan Hassan to finish third and earn the coveted Olympic medal, becoming the first U.S. woman to earn a medal in the 1500 meter.

Questions For Thought:

1. Jenny Simpson switched from an event in which she held the American record. How do you get out of your comfort zone?
2. Jenny considers herself a predator. Do you consider yourself a predator when it comes to competing?
3. The Olympic final brought out the best in Jenny. She ran the last 800 meters faster than her 800 PR. What brings out the best in you?

Christian Taylor

Double Gold Medalist

Christian Taylor went into the Rio Olympics as the favorite. After all, he won the event four years ago at the 2012 London Olympics and had dominated the competition in the last four years. Christian has consistently been close—only inches away—to the triple jump world record held by Jonathan Edwards. Christian's Olympic goal was to repeat as the gold medalist and set the Olympic record and world record.

Christian has a fan club that sits next to the pit as he triple jumps. He energizes himself as he shouts "right now!" and stares down the runway visualizing every step, imagining every movement. While still staring, he continues to energize himself by clapping his hands over his head to get the crowd involved. As the crowd begins to clap, he feels the energy from them.

Christian's first jump in the Olympic triple jump of 58-7 ¼ took the lead. His second jump of 58-3 ¼ was good but still almost more than a foot and a half away from the world record. He fouled on his third jump and on his fourth jump matched his second attempt, before fouling again on his fifth.

Down to his final attempt at a new world record Christian had the gold medal already won, but he wanted more. He shouted to the crowd, "One more! One more!" He began his energization routine. Visualization. Clap. Yell. He could feel the energy surging through him. He felt this was the time and place to take the world record. Down the runway he ran, accelerating to build speed, smooth and fluid, he hit the board and took off. His hop phase was low and fast, his step phase was a smooth glide and his jump phase was powerful. He landed past the yellow world record line. For a brief second it seemed like the world record belonged to Christian Taylor. But, the red flag went up, a foul.

The disappointment of not breaking the record faded quickly. You can break the world record any time, but the Olympics only come along once every four years. Christian cried for joy on the medal podium, as he had won his second straight gold medal, becoming the first triple jumper in 40 years to repeat, and the first American to do it since 1904.

Questions For Thought:

1. Christian's philosophy is "leave it all out there." What does that philosophy mean to you?
2. Christian dominates his event but continues to motivate himself. How do you motivate yourself?
3. Christian uses a mental routine to achieve his proper arousal zone before he jumps. Do you have a mental routine? What would it take to develop one?

Wayde van Niekerk

World Record Wayde

When Wayde van Niekerk ran the fourth-fastest time in history at the 2015 World Championships in Beijing, running 43.48 to take down defending champion LaShawn Merritt, the world was shocked. But Wayde was just getting started.

Wayde was a fighter from the start. Born in South Africa in 1992, he arrived 11 weeks early and weighed just twice the weight of what his future Olympic gold medal would weigh. His mother was warned he might not make it, or at best, be disabled. His mother, Odessa Swarts, was a world-class athlete as a teen. South Africa was violently transitioning from apartheid to democracy, and she chose to oppose apartheid by participating in South African Council on Sport (SACOS) events. During South Africa's isolation, the country's athletes were banned from international competition, and participation in SACOS events was a form of passive resistance. Though Odessa ran a 12.32 100 and a 25.3 200 at age 16 on a clay track, her chances as a black female athlete of achieving world-wide recognition were slim.

But her son has been able to compete on a world stage representing a democratic South Africa. The South African sprinter not only won a gold medal in Rio, but he obliterated a 17-year-old world record, running 43.03 seconds. The previous world record of 43.18 was set by two-time Olympic gold medalist Michael Johnson in 1999.

The most amazing part was that Wayde not only won but set a world record out of lane eight, a hard feat as the other competitors remain out of sight for almost the entire race. It can be difficult to gauge speed and position in lane eight, but it didn't bother Wayde—instead it gave him motivation. And his coach, Anna Sofia Botha, a 74-year-old great-grandmother, wasn't bothered, as "every lane is the same distance."

Wayde started working with Botha after the 2012 Olympic year when he began his studies at the University of the Free State in Bloemfontein, South Africa. She's been the head coach of track and field there since 1990. Wayde credits his success to his coach's strict regime that keeps him disciplined and focused on the goal. With a world record and Olympic gold already in his hands, the sky is the limit.

Questions For Thought:

1. Wayde's mother helped set the stage for black South African athletes. Have you ever set the stage for big things to come?
2. Wayde won Olympic gold and set a world record out of lane 8, which is very difficult to do. Have you ever achieved something others deem impossible or a disadvantage?
3. Wayde's coach is a 74-year-old great-grandmother. Does success have an age limit?

Shelbi Vaughan

Throw Queen

Shelbi Vaughan has gone through a series of nicknames: "Barbie," "The Hammer," "The Throw Princess." What's next? She hopes it's "The Throw Queen."

She grew up a girly-girl who always had on a dress, a full face of makeup, tanned skin, and blonde hair. She began throwing the discus in seventh grade and went on to set the national high school discus record by nearly two feet and break the American Junior discus record twice. She topped the national high school discus list by 26 feet and became the first field event athlete to be unanimously selected as the 2012 Girls Athlete of the Year by Track & Field News. As a 17-year-old high school senior, she finished 4th in the 2012 U.S. Olympic Trials, missing a team berth by less than 2 feet.

Shelbi originally went to Texas A&M to play volleyball and compete in track and field. After two years, she made the decision to focus on track, adding two new implements to her resume—the indoor weight and the hammer—to enhance her discus performance.

Shelbi came into the 2016 Olympic Trials following a disappointing sixth-place performance at the NCAA Championships, where she was the two-time defending champion. A couple of adjustments during training for the Olympic Trials helped restore her confidence. A throw of 197-9 in the second round gave her second place and a spot on the Olympic team.

In Rio, rain delayed competition for half an hour. When competition resumed, the throwers had little time to warm-up, and Shelbi ended up throwing off her sweats at the last minute to throw. The chaos frazzled Shelbi, and she even hit a photographer as her throw went out of bounds. Her last two throws went 174-11 and 153-3, well short of her career-best of 211-8 and her season-best of 199-3. As the second-youngest competitor in the field, Shelbi Vaughan left Rio with a 29th place finish and Olympic experience to propel her for the future and upgrade her royalty status to "The Throw Queen."

Questions For Thought:

1. Shelbi just missed the Olympic team in 2012 but rebounded to make it four years later. How long are you willing to make a commitment?
2. Although Shelbi was not throwing well before the Trials, she made adjustments. Have you ever made adjustments that paid off?
3. Does your nickname exemplify what you do or stand for?

Jared Ward

Accidental Marathoner

Jared Ward was considered a surprise qualifier when he made the U.S Olympic Team in the marathon by placing third. He knew it would take a personal best to place among the elite runners in the 2016 Olympic Games in Rio. Ward rose to the challenge running a personal-best time of 2 hours, 11 minutes, 30 seconds to finish in sixth place. The performance accomplished his goal of a top-10 Olympic finish in only his fifth marathon.

Jared ran with the leaders for the first 16 miles of the Olympic marathon but felt his legs tighten up and get heavy as he began to drop back from the front pack. However, Jared completed his master's thesis on marathon pacing and he patiently waited for his second wind as he practiced his mental skills with positive self-talk. Soon, Jared was back in his rhythm and discovered he still had some fuel in the tank. He began to pass runners, working his way back into the top-10 as he drew closer to the finish line. The numerous hours of the mental and physical training came together as Jared dug down deep and tapped into an extra reserve.

Jared ended up a marathon runner by unfortunate circumstances. When he returned from serving a missionary trip in 2009, it was too late to enroll in Brigham Young University's fall semester and run cross-country with his team. He entered a fun run, but because it was timed and organized, the NCAA ruled that would cost him a collegiate season. Although the decision was eventually reversed in 2014 it meant he had to try to find another purpose in his training and he trained for the Chicago Marathon.

Jared Ward proved that sometimes events that seem like heartaches at the onset but can be blessings in disguise.

Questions For Thought:

1. What blessings in disguise have you had?
2. Jared didn't give up in the Olympic Marathon and was able to finish strong. Are there points in a competition you feel like giving up? How do you work through that feeling?
3. How do you find the extra reserve you have in your tank?

Novlene Williams-Mills

Cancer Survivor

Jamaican Novlene Williams-Mills received devastating news exactly one month before the 2012 London Olympics: she had breast cancer. Her sister had died in 2010 at age 38 due to ovarian cancer. Novlene made the decision to hold off surgery until after the Olympics, and later that week she ran 50.60 to secure her place in the 400 meter for the London Games. She finished fifth in the Olympic 400 final and helped her country claim the 4x400 meter relay bronze.

Three days after the Games, she underwent surgery to remove a small lump from her breast. A double mastectomy was to follow before a further operation to cut out the remaining cancerous cells, as well as reconstructive surgery.

After an Olympic bronze medal in London soon after receiving a breast cancer diagnosis, Novlene thought she could mentally overcome any future obstacle. But her body threw her a new curveball in the months leading up to the 2015 World Championships in Beijing. It was diagnosed as a thyroid infection, but a tiny gland in her throat left her wanting to leave the sport, having lost confidence in her body.

Her confidence returned in Beijing when, with 50 meters to go, she caught Francena McCorory of the U.S. and brought Jamaica home to their first 4x400 gold in 14 years.

At the age of 34, Novlene knew 2016 would be her fourth and last shot at the Olympics. She viewed the Games as her second chance—focusing not on cancer, but the race ahead and enjoying the moment. Going into the 4x400 finals, Novlene knew it would be a close battle between Jamaica and the U.S. Although the U.S. edged out for the victory, Novlene Williams-Mills anchored her country with a 50.52 split to a silver medal, her fourth consecutive medal in the event.

Questions For Thought:

1. Novlene has overcome cancer and gone out to compete at the highest level. Do your challenges in life seem minor compared to what Novlene endured?
2. Novlene believes she can mentally overcome any future obstacle. How could you develop this type of mental toughness?
3. Novlene likes the pressure of running anchor when the team depends on her to "bring it home." Do you like to "bring it home?"

Rudy Winkler

Waiting for the Call

Rudy Winkler was on his way to a meet in El Salvador to compete in the hammer throw when he got an email from USA Track & Field notifying him he would be competing in the Olympic Games. It's not the way most athletes discover they'd made it to the Olympic Games. Rudy won the 2016 U.S. Olympic Trials with a throw of 251-10, but had not met the Olympic standard of 252-7, as had no one else in the competition. Since he did not receive an automatic bid to the Olympics, he had to rely on one of 24 invitations to Rio from the International Association of Athletics Federations, the governing body of track and field.

Rudy attended Cornell and tore his meniscus in his right knee weightlifting, forcing him to miss his entire first year. He never lost his drive to win and as a sophomore, Rudy was a first team All-American, an Ivy League champion in the weight indoor and hammer outdoor, and set a new school record in weight and hammer, among multiple academic awards. He was the NCAA runner-up in the hammer outdoors in 2016 after placing eighth in 2015. When Rudy won the hammer throw at the 2016 United States Olympic Trials, he was surprised to win against some of the best athletes in the sport but not surprised by his throw of 251-10, more than five feet further than the competition.

Rudy waited nearly a week to receive his invitation to the Rio Games. Since only 22 athletes hit the Olympic standard and the International Olympic Committee would accept 32 total throwers, Rudy remained in contention for one of the final 10 spots. When he got the invitation, he trained through the meet in El Salvador and set his sights on Rio.

Rudy's first and third attempts at the Olympic Games hit the net, and his throw of 235-10 ¼ wasn't enough to put him in the final. He finished eighth in his flight and 18th overall, when just 12 would advance to the final. Only the eventual winner, Wojciech Nowicki of Poland, threw farther than Rudy had at the Trials.

Rudy, who got an early start at age 14 throwing the hammer in upstate New York, competed in his first Olympics at age 21 and has many years to throw his way to the top.

Questions For Thought:

1. Rudy had to wait to find out whether or not he would compete at the Olympics. How hard is it to stay calm and focused while waiting for news that could determine your future?
2. Rudy competed against former Olympians at the Trials but came out on top. How have you stepped up to the plate against tough competition?
3. Rudy was on his way to another meet when he heard he would go to the Olympics but was able to adapt his training and mindset. Can you adapt according to your circumstances?

Julius Yego

YouTube Yego

The country of Kenya has become an Olympic power in track and field, establishing a legendary tradition in the middle-distance and distance events. However, prior to the 2016 Olympic Games, no Kenyan had ever won an Olympic medal in a throwing event.

Julius Yego grew up in Kenya, a country that placed very little emphasis on the field events. Julius was self-motivated to learn to throw the javelin and taught himself by watching the throwing technique of world record holder Jan Zelezný of Czech Republic on YouTube. Slowly, Julius began to improve and he looked forward to the challenge of competing against the best in the world. However, Kenya declined to enter him for the 2008 World Junior Championships. Julius's dream of competing at a world-class level was shattered, but he overcame the major disappointment and began to train even harder. He made the Kenyan Olympic team and finished 12th in the 2012 London Olympics. He continued his meteoric rise from obscurity to global stardom as he won the 2015 Track and Field World Championships in the javelin.

During the 2016 track and field season, Julius was hampered by an ankle injury that had become increasingly unreliable. In the qualifying round of the javelin at Rio, he failed to throw well in his first two attempts in the qualifying round. The pressure was on, and Julius responded to the challenge by finally earning a spot in the javelin final on his last throw. In the final, Julius got off to a great start and took the lead after the first throw, throwing an impressive 289-6. On throw number two, Julius fouled and injured his ankle in the process. With his ankle hurting, Julius passed in round three, as he still had the lead. In round four, Julius tried to throw but fouled again and with blood coming from his ankle, he withdrew from the competition by passing in rounds five and six.

Julius could only watch the final two throws as Thomas Rohler of Germany overtook him in round five by throwing 296-3 for the win with Julius forced to settle for second place. As Julius was transported in a wheelchair for treatment, tears flowed down his cheeks; his gold medal hopes had flowed away.

Despite the unfortunate injury, Julius Yego captured the first-ever Olympic medal for Kenya in the javelin to add to the fairytale of the self-taught javelin thrower.

Questions For Thought:

1. Julius Yego was motivated to learn more about the javelin. What things do you wish to learn more about?
2. What motivates you to learn more? How do you go about learning more?
3. Kenya did not have a tradition in the throws, but Julius was determined to start one. How could you part of a new tradition?

Resources

ABC News 4. (2016, August 12). Raven Saunders finishes 5th in Rio; Michelle Carter takes gold. Retrieved from http://abcnews4.com/news/local/raven-saunders-headed-for-gold-at-rio-olympics

Abulleil, R. (2015, August 17). Inside story: How Mutaz Barshim took the leap into stardom. *Sport 360.* Retrieved from http://sport360.com/article/athletics/40949/inside-story-how-mutaz-barshim-took-leap-stardom

Agence France Presse. (2016, July 6). Dope ban hammer thrower Gwen Berry headed to Rio Olympics. *Yahoo Sports.* Retrieved from http://sports.yahoo.com/news/dope-ban-hammer-thrower-gwen-berry-headed-rio-021238311--oly.html

Amato, L. (2016, July 25). Dalilah Muhammad takes the fast lane to Rio. *Times Ledger.* Retrieved from http://www.timesledger.com/stories/2016/30/dalilahmuhammadolympics_2016_07_22_q.html

Amick, S. (2016, August 12). Women's 10,000: Ayana smashes world record; Huddle sets U.S. record. *USA Today.* Retrieved from http://www.usatoday.com/story/sports/olympics/rio-2016/2016/08/12/womens-10000-rio-olympics-almaz-ayana-world-record-molly-huddle/88611530/

Archdeacon, T. (2016, July 16). Darke County's Clayton Murphy an Olympian now and forever. *myDayton Daily News.* Retrieved from http://www.mydaytondailynews.com/news/sports/tom-archdeacon-murphy-an-olympian-now-and-forever/nrzFB/

Armour, N. (2016, July 23). Tatyana McFadden to tackle seven events in Rio Paralympics. *USA Today.* Retrieved from http://www.usatoday.com/story/sports/olympics/rio-2016/2016/07/21/tatyana-mcfadden-tackle-seven-events-rio-paralympics/87411432/

Ashford, B. (2016, August 16). Jenny Simpson makes Olympics history as she wins bronze in women's 1,500m - but fellow American Shannon Rowbury just misses out following 2012 heartache. *Daily Mail.* Retrieved from http://www.dailymail.co.uk/news/article-3744466/Olympics-Athletics-Kenyan-Kipyegon-takes-womens-1-500m-gold.html#ixzz4IAgiWwJt

Ask Listen Learn. (n.d.). Christian Taylor. Retrieved from http://asklistenlearn.org/superstars/christian-taylor/

Associated Press. (2016, August 12). Lutz resident Tianna Bartoletta won her Women's 100m heat. *WFLA.* Retrieved from http://wfla.com/2016/08/12/lutz-resident-tianna-bartoletta-won-her-womens-100m-heat/

Associated Press. (2016, August 16). Will Claye wins Olympic silver, proposes to girlfriend. *NBC Olympics.* Retrieved from http://www.nbcolympics.com/news/will-claye-wins-olympic-silver-proposes-girlfriend

Associated Press. (2016, July 5). Greg Rutherford risks permanent hearing loss if he continues competing. *The Guardian.* Retrieved from https://www.theguardian.com/sport/2016/jul/05/greg-rutherford-olympic-champion-hearing-loss?

Associated Press. (2016, June 29). Trayvon Bromell not afraid of top sprinters. *NBC Olympics.* Retrieved from http://www.nbcolympics.com/news/trayvon-bromell-not-afraid-top-sprinters

Associated Press. (2016, March 12). Scandals force Shannon Rowbury to relive Olympic disappointment. *NBC Olympics.* Retrieved from http://www.nbcolympics.com/news/scandals-force-shannon-rowbury-relive-olympic-disappointment

Associated Press. (2016, September 9). Tatyana McFadden's bid for seven golds at Paralympics falls short with silver in 100. *The Baltimore Sun.* Retrieved from http://www.baltimoresun.com/sports/olympics/bal-tatyana-mcfadden-s-bid-for-seven-golds-at-paralympics-falls-short-with-silver-in-100-20160909-story.html

Barker, S. (2016, August 18). Wayde Van Niekerk's run was historic in at least four ways. *Deadspin.* Retrieved from http://deadspin.com/wayde-van-niekerks-run-was-historic-in-at-least-four-wa-1785325792

Barker, S. (2016, July 7). U.S. Olympic Committee tells Oiselle to delete social media posts, ignores others. *Deadspin.* Retrieved from http://fittish.deadspin.com/u-s-olympic-committee-tells-oiselle-to-delete-social-m-1783304825

Barton, O. (2016, July 22). #Rock2Rio with American record-breaking hammer thrower Gwen Berry. *RockTape*. Retrieved from http://www.rocktape.com/rock2rio-with-american-record-breaking-hammer-thrower-gwen-berry/

BBC. (2012, August 4). Greg Rutherford wins Olympic long jump gold for Great Britain. Retrieved from http://www.bbc.com/sport/olympics/18912032

BBC. (2016, August 15). Rio Olympics 2016: Usain Bolt wins 100m gold, Justin Gatlin second. Retrieved from http://www.bbc.com/sport/olympics/36689475

Bell, C. (2016, August 14). The story of Caterine Ibargüen: Colombian Olympic gold medalist. *See Colombia*. Retrieved from http://seecolombia.travel/blog/2016/08/the-story-of-caterine-ibarguen-colombian-olympic-gold-medalist/

Bellino, M. (2015, May 7). Boris Berian: From McDonald's to 800m U.S. lead. *FloTrack*. Retrieved from http://www.flotrack.org/article/31371-boris-berian-from-mcdonald-s-to-800m-u-s-lead

Bellino, M. (2016, August 18). Kate Grace runs 1:58 PB, advances to the Olympic 800m final. *FloTrack*. Retrieved from http://www.flotrack.org/article/45278-kate-grace-runs-1-58-pb-advances-to-the-olympic-800m-final

Bellino, M. (2016, August 26). Gabe Grunewald is having cancer surgery today. *FloTrack*. Retrieved from http://www.flotrack.org/article/45590-gabe-grunewald-is-having-cancer-surgery-today

Bellino, M. (2016, July 2). Donavan Brazier protested 800m prelim and was denied. *FloTrack*. Retrieved from http://www.flotrack.org/article/43192-donavan-brazier-protested-800m-prelim-and-was-denied

Berg, N. (2016, July 8). Keturah Orji clinches Olympic berth at U.S. Track trials. *The Red & Black*. Retrieved from http://www.redandblack.com/sports/keturah-orji-clinches-olympic-berth-at-u-s-track-trials/article_21e79978-44c2-11e6-8191-7b429750f720.html

Bieler, D. (2016, August 14). South Africa's Wayde van Niekerk sets world record, wins gold in men's 400 meters. *The Washington Post*. Retrieved from https://www.washingtonpost.com/olympics/2016/live-updates/rio-games/scores-and-latest-news/south-africas-wayde-van-niekerk-sets-world-record-wins-gold-in-mens-400-meters/

Blount, R. (2016, August 16). Former Gophers runner Ben Blankenship qualifies for 1,500-meter semifinals. *StarTribune*. Retrieved from http://www.startribune.com/foirmer-gopher-ben-blankenshhip-to-run-1-500-on-tuesday/390257931/

Blount, R. (2016, August 20). Hassan Mead slips to 11th in men's 5,000 meters final in Rio; Mo Farah has double-double. *StarTribune*. Retrieved from http://www.startribune.com/hassan-mead-slips-to-12th-in-men-s-5-000-meters-final-in-rio/390816411/

Blount, R. (2016, May 11). Ben Blankenship mixing business and pleasure in Thursday's TC 1 Mile. *StarTribune*. Retrieved from http://www.startribune.com/ben-blankenship-mixing-business-and-pleasure-in-thursday-s-tc-1-mile/379074261/

Borzilleri, M. (2016, June 15). Road to Rio: Temple's Ajee Wilson uses her moment of zen for victory. *American Sports Network*. Retrieved from http://americansportsnet.com/road-to-rio-temples-ajee-wilson-uses-her-moment-of-zen-for-victory/

Brady, J. (2016, July 10). US Track & Field Olympic trial results: Allyson Felix misses out in 200-meter finals on last day of trials. *SB Nation*. Retrieved from http://www.sbnation.com/2016/7/10/12144462/2016-olympics-trials-results-track-field-usa-allyson-felix

Brant, J. (2016, August 8). Can Galen Rupp win an Olympic marathon medal? *Runner's World*. Retrieved from http://www.runnersworld.com/olympics/can-galen-rupp-win-an-olympic-marathon-medal\

Brown, B. (2016, August 15). Philly and NJ's Nia Ali overcomes hurdles on and off the track on her road to Rio. *NBC 10*. Retrieved from http://www.nbcphiladelphia.com/news/local/10-Questions-100-Meter-Hurdles-Olympics-Nia-Ali-Philadelphia-389318742.html

Brown, O. (2016, March 19). Olympic champion and world record breaker Aries Merritt on track to complete remarkable comeback after transplant. *The Telegraph*. Retrieved from http://www.telegraph.co.uk/athletics/2016/03/19/olympic-champion-and-world-record-breaker-aries-merritt-on-track/

Bull, A. (2016, August 16). Brazil's Thiago Braz da Silva elevated to national hero status after pole vault gold. *The Guardian*. Retrieved from https://www.theguardian.com/sport/2016/aug/16/brazilthiago-braz-da-silva-elevated-to-national-hero-status-after-pole-vault-gold

Burfoot, A. (2016, July 1). Men's 10,000 meters: Rupp wins with huge sprint at finish. *Runner's World*. Retrieved from http://www.runnersworld.com/olympic-trials/the-us-olympic-trials-mens-10000-meters

Burfoot, A. (2016, July 14). How an Ohio pig farm raised an Olympian. *Runner's World*. Retrieved from http://www.runnersworld.com/olympic-trials/how-an-ohio-pig-farm-raised-an-olympian

Butler, S. (2016, August 21). Meb's final games: A fall and a flourish. *Runner's World*. Retrieved from http://www.runnersworld.com/olympics/mebs-final-games-a-fall-and-a-flourish

Caple, J. (2016, July 7). Will Claye keeps Rio hopes alive in triple jump prelims. *ESPN*. Retrieved from http://espn.go.com/olympics/trackandfield/story/_/id/16876174/olympic-track-trials-2016-claye-keeps-rio-hopes-alive-triple-jump-prelims

Caple, J. (2016, July 7). Will Claye keeps Rio hopes alive in triple jump prelims. *ESPN*. Retrieved from http://www.espn.com/olympics/trackandfield/story/_/id/16876174/olympic-track-trials-2016-claye-keeps-rio-hopes-alive-triple-jump-prelims

Caples, J. (2016, July 10). Aries Merritt's improbably journey. *ESPN*. Retrieved from http://www.espn.com/espn/feature/story/_/id/16942497/how-aries-merritt-recovered-kidney-transplant-reach-olympic-trials

CBS News. (2016, August 21). Meb Keflezighi: The long run. Retrieved from http://www.cbsnews.com/news/meb-keflezighi-the-long-run/

Chapin, J. (2016, July 24). Tri-Village grad latest local to live Olympic dream. *Pal-Item*. Retrieved from http://www.pal-item.com/story/sports/2016/07/23/tri-village-grad-latest-local-live-olympic-dream/87274196/

Chavez, C. (2015, August 29). Ashton Eaton breaks his own decathlon world record; wins gold. *Sports Illustrated*. Retrieved from http://www.si.com/more-sports/2015/08/28/ashton-eaton-decathlon-world-record-track-and-field-world-championships-beijing-results

Chavez, C. (2016, August 12). Ethiopia's Almaz Ayana wins gold with new women's 10,000-meter world record. *Sports Illustrated*. Retrieved from http://www.si.com/olympics/2016/08/12/almaz-ayana-world-record-rio-2016-olympics-10000-meters-molly-huddle

Chavez, C. (2016, July 11). Allyson Felix fails to make 200-meter team, can't get Olympic double. *Sports Illustrated*. Retrieved from http://www.si.com/olympics/2016/07/10/allyson-felix-200-meters-video-tori-bowie-us-olympic-trials

Corbitt, K. (2016, July 7). Erik Kynard, former K-State All-American, resumes quest for Olympic gold at U.S. Trials. *The Topeka Capital-Journal*. Retrieved from http://cjonline.com/sports/catzone/2016-07-07/erik-kynard-former-k-state-all-american-resumes-quest-olympic-gold-us#

Cotton, C. (2016, October 6). Rudy Winkler: From the farm to the Olympics. *The Cornell Daily Sun*. Retrieved from http://cornellsun.com/2016/10/06/rudy-winkler-from-the-farm-to-the-olympics/

Cox, C. (2015, August 28). Ibargüen: That dominant athlete you haven't heard of. *Aljazeera*. Retrieved from http://www.aljazeera.com/news/2015/08/ibarguen-dominant-athlete-haven-heard-150827200450879.html

Crouse, K. (2016, August 15). This great-grandmother coaches an Olympic champion. Now let her by. *The New York Times*. Retrieved from http://www.nytimes.com/2016/08/16/sports/olympics/wayde-van-niekerk-coach-anna-sofia-botha.html?_r=0

Crumpacker, J. (2016, July 10). Will Claye, Christian Taylor earn return trips to Olympics in men's triple jump. *The Register-Guard*. Retrieved from http://registerguard.com/rg/sports/34560681-81/will-claye-christian-taylor-earn-return-trips-to-olympics-in-mens-triple-jump.html.csp

Dennehy, C. (2015, July 6). Despite Fall, Evan Jager breaks U.S. steeplechase record. *Runner's World*. Retrieved from http://www.runnersworld.com/racing/despite-fall-evan-jager-breaks-us-steeplechase-record

Dennehy, C. (2016, August 13). Record run in Rio just the start for Ayana. *IAAF*. Retrieved from https://www.iaaf.org/news/feature/almaz-ayana-olympics-2016-ethiopia

Donaldson, A. (2016, February 13). Former BYU, Davis High runner Jared Ward earns spot on U.S. Olympic team. *Deseret News Sports*. Retrieved from http://www.deseretnews.com/article/765684363/Rupp-Cragg-win-marathon-trial-earn-spot-on-US-Olympic-Team.html

Dutch, T. (2016, August 19). Donavan Brazier to train with Duane Solomon and Johnny Gray. *FloTrack*. Retrieved from http://www.flotrack.org/article/45314-donavan-brazier-to-train-with-duane-solomon-and-johnny-gray

Dutch, T. (2016, July 2). Duane Solomon, Donavan Brazier out in Olympic Trials first round. *FloTrack*. Retrieved from http://www.flotrack.org/article/43189-duane-solomon-donavan-brazier-out-in-olympic-trials-first-round

Dutch, T. (2016, July 28). Coach Floreal shares how Keni Harrison went from heartbreak to world record. *FloTrack*. Retrieved from http://www.flotrack.org/article/44164-coach-floreal-shares-how-keni-harrison-went-from-heartbreak-to-world-record

Dutch, T. (2016, September 9). Sandi Morris becomes second to clear 5.00m outdoors. *FloTrack*. Retrieved from http://www.flotrack.org/article/46044-sandi-morris-becomes-second-woman-to-clear-5-00m-outdoors

Eder, L. (2015, August 25). Emma Coburn: Ready to step up, will talented US steeple star climb podium? *Colorado Running*. Retrieved from http://www.coloradorunnermag.com/2015/08/25/emma-coburn-ready-to-step-up-will-talented-us-steeple-star-climb-podium/

Elliot, H. (2016, August 27). Rio Olympics: Justin Gatlin defends his past, moves forward in men's 100. *Los Angeles Times*. Retrieved from http://www.latimes.com/sports/olympics/la-sp-oly-rio-2016-gatlin-defends-his-past-moves-forward-1471107703-htmlstory.html

Elliot, H. (2016, July 28). English Gardner is going to be much more than a name that you can't forget. *Los Angeles Times*. Retrieved from http://www.latimes.com/sports/la-sp-oly-track-english-gardner-20160727-snap-story.html

Engle, C. (2014, August 15). A candid interview with Gabriele Grunewald. *Runner's World*. Retrieved from http://www.runnersworld.com/elite-runners/a-candid-interview-with-gabriele-grunewald

Esquire Middle East. (2016, August 17). Qatar's Mutaz Barshim wins Olympic silver. Retrieved from http://www.esquireme.com/content/17321-qatars-mutaz-barshim-wins-olympic-silver

Felicien, B. (2016, August 19). Greenville's Sandi Morris is an Olympic medalist. *Greenville Online*. Retrieved from http://www.greenvilleonline.com/story/sports/2016/08/19/live-sandi-morris-competing-pole-vault-finals/88994710/

Fox, K. (2016, August 12). 6 incredible stats from the fastest women's 10,000-meter race in history. *Runner's World*. Retrieved from http://www.runnersworld.com/olympics/6-incredible-stats-from-the-fastest-womens-10000-meter-race-in-history

Frederick, J, (2016, August 12). Mendota Heights heptathlete Heather Miller-Koch is now a believer. *TwinCities.com Pioneer Press*. Retrieved from http://www.twincities.com/2016/08/11/mendota-heights-heptathlete-heather-miller-koch-is-now-a-believer/

Frederick, J. (2016, August 15). Olympics: Stillwater's Ben Blankenship takes his job seriously. *TwinCities.Com Pioneer Press*. Retrieved from http://www.twincities.com/2016/08/15/olympics-stillwaters-ben-blankenship-takes-his-job-seriously/

Frederick, J. (2016, August 17). Olympics: After review, Hassan Mead advances to 5K final. *TwinCities.com Pioneer Press*. Retrieved from http://www.twincities.com/2016/08/17/olympics-after-review-hassan-mead-advances-to-5k-final/

Gaffey, C. (2016, August 16). Who is David Rudisha, Kenya's double Olympic champion? *Newsweek*. Retrieved from http://www.newsweek.com/who-david-rudisha-kenyas-and-double-olympic-champion-490689

Germano, S. (2016, July 11). Sydney McLaughlin, 16, hurdles her way to the Olympics. *The Wall Street Journal*. Retrieved from http://www.wsj.com/articles/sydney-mclaughlin-16-hurdles-her-way-to-the-olympics-1468271857

Germano, S. (2016, July 9). Aries Merritt narrowly misses out on Olympic hurdles spot. *The Wall Street Journal*. Retrieved from http://www.wsj.com/articles/aries-merritt-narrowly-misses-out-on-olympic-hurdles-spot-1468121651

Goodwin, C. (2016, July 20). Columbus native Miller-Koch takes talents to Rio. *WKOW*. Retrieved from http://www.wkow.com/story/32494272/2016/07/Wednesday/columbus-native-miller-koch-takes-talents-to-rio

Graney, E. (2016, July 2). Vashti Cunningham's athletic gifts also can be traced to mother. *Review Journal*. Retrieved from http://www.reviewjournal.com/opinion/columns-blogs/ed-graney/vashti-cunningham-s-athletic-gifts-also-can-be-traced-mother

Gregorian, V. (2016, August 15). Four years ahead of schedule, UMKC's Courtney Frerichs finishes 11th in Olympic steeplechase. *The Kansas City Star*. Retrieved from http://www.kansas city.com/sports/spt-columns-blogs/vahe-gregorian/article95855992.html

Hambleton, K. (2016, July 17). Maggie Malone: From Geneva to Rio, on the trip of her life. *Lincoln Journal Star*. Retrieved from http://journalstar.com/sports/olympics/maggie-malone-from-geneva-to-rio-on-the-trip-of/article_22c65de5-81b7-5f4a-8d7c-70b3b039016f.html

Hartsell, J. (2016, August 5). Community helps send Saunders to Rio Games. *The Post and Courier*. Retrieved from http://www.postandcourier.com/20160806/160809589/for-olympian-raven-saunders-many-people-paved-the-road-to-rio

Hefferman, T. (2016, July 7). Former Saluki Raven Saunders earns spot on Team USA. *The Southern Illinoisan*. Retrieved from http://thesouthern.com/sports/former-saluki-raven-saunders-earns-spot-on-team-usa/article_aae856d8-0957-505b-980d-3743e95e41af.html

Helling, S. (2016, August 15). Allyson Felix takes silver in 400-meter dash after Shaunae Miller's dramatic finish line dive. *People Magazine*. Retrieved from http://people.com/sports/rio-olympics-shaunae-miller-dives-to-finish-line-in-400-meter-dash/

Hendrix, D. (2016). Finishing the race: Winter Garden resident brings home silver medal from fourth and final Olympic Games. *Orange Observer*. Retrieved from http://www.orange observer.com/article/finishing-race-winter-garden-resident-brings-home-silver-medal-fourth-and-final-olympic

Henley, B. (2016, June 22). Novlene Williams-Mills: 'I had completely lost confidence in my body.' *ESPN*. Retrieved from http://www.espn.com/espnw/voices/article/16432407/novlene-williams-mills-had-completely-lost-confidence-my-body

Hine, C. (2016, August 17). Algonquin's Evan Jager wins silver: 'It was indescribable.' *Chicago Tribune*. Retrieved from http://www.chicagotribune.com/sports/international/ct-evan-jager-silver-steeplechase-olympics-20160817-story.html

Hussein, A. (2016). Julius Yego heartbroken after injury ends his gold medal dream. *Tuko*. Retrieved from https://tuko.co.ke/176631-julius-yego-finally-wins-medal-rio-olympics-heartbreak.html

Ingle, S. (2016, August 15). David Rudisha retains Olympic 800m title with 'greatest moment of career.' *The Guardian*. Retrieved from https://www.theguardian.com/sport/2016/aug/16/athletics-david-rudisha-olympic-800m-title

Ingle, S. (2016, August 20). Magical Mo Farah bags another Olympic gold and earns his place in history. *The Guardian*. Retrieved from https://www.theguardian.com/sport/2016/aug/20/mo-farah-gold-medal-5000m-double-double-history

International Association Athletics Federations. (2015, August 25). Report: Men's 400m final—IAAF World Championships, Beijing 2015. Retrieved from https://www.iaaf.org/news/report/beijing-2015-men-400m-final

International Association of Athletics Federations. (n.d.). Rules and regulations. Retrieved from https://www.iaaf.org/about-iaaf/documents/rules-regulations

Jackson-Gibson, A. (2016, July 7). Pole vaulter Sandi Morris is ready to fly at Olympic trials. *Excelle Sports*. Retrieved from http://www.excellesports.com/news/sandi-morris-olympic-trials-rio/

Jennings, C. (2016, July 9). Football can wait: Oregon's Devon Allen off to Rio Games. *ESPN*. Retrieved from http://espn.go.com/olympics/trackandfield/story/_/id/16941112/oregon-ducks-devon-allen-wins-olympic-track-trials-110-meter-hurdles-reach-rio-games

Kamrani, C. (2016, August 21). Olympics: Utahn Jared Ward runs race of his life, finishes 6th in Rio marathon. *The Salt Lake Tribune.* Retrieved from http://www.sltrib.com/home/4262680-155/olympics-byus-jared-ward-finishes-6th?page=2

Kaufman, M. (2013, August 21). Northwestern alumna Brianna Rollins hurdles adversity to become the best. *Miami Herald.* Retrieved from http://www.miamiherald.com/sports/high-school/prep-miami-dade/article1954294.html

Keegan, T. (2016, July 17). Olympian Geubelle overcomes adversity. *Lawrence Journal-World.* Retrieved from http://www2.ljworld.com/news/2016/jul/17/tom-keegan-olympian-geubelle-overcomes-adversity/

Kilgore, A. (2016, August 1). Matthew Centrowitz follows his father's footsteps to a second Olympic team. *The Washington Post.* Retrieved from https://www.washingtonpost.com/sports/olympics/matthew-centrowitz-follows-his-fathers-footsteps-to-a-second-olympics/2016/08/01/d65a792c-4f79-11e6-a422-83ab49ed5e6a_story.html

Kilgore, A. (2016, August 16). U.S. track star Kerron Clement appeared in a Beyoncé video. *The Washington Post.* Retrieved from https://www.washingtonpost.com/olympics/2016/live-updates/rio-games/scores-and-latest-news/u-s-track-star-kerron-clement-appeared-in-a-beyonce-video/

Kines, M. (2016, August 12). Ethiopian runner Almaz Ayana stuns crowd with 10,000-meter world record. *ESPNW.* Retrieved from http://www.espn.com/espnw/voices/article/17286920/ethiopian-runner-almaz-ayana-stuns-olympic-crowd-10000-meter-world-record

Kissane, J. (2011, October 28). Hassan Mead's wild ride. *Runner's World.* Retrieved from http://www.runnersworld.com/college/hassan-meads-wild-ride

Kitching, C. (2016, August 18). The medal is just for her': Touching moment long jump hero brings his gold home to his Alzheimer's-stricken mom. *Daily Mail.* Retrieved from http://www.daily mail.co.uk/news/article-3746634/Jeff-Henderson-brings-gold-medal-home-mom-Alzheimer-s.html#ixzz4NaSgeDJx

Knight, M. (2016). How family helped this Olympian overcome a devastating loss. *Real Simple.* Retrieved from http://www.realsimple.com/work-life/alysia-montano-mom

Koon, D. (2016, August 19). Striking gold: A chat with Olympic medalist Jeff Henderson. *Arkansas Times.* Retrieved from http://www.arktimes.com/ArkansasBlog/archives/2016/08/19/striking-gold-a-chat-with-olympic-medalist-jeff-henderson

KU Athletics. (2016, August 13). Jayhawk Olympians compete Saturday in Rio. Retrieved from http://www.kuathletics.com/news/2016/8/13/track-field-jayhawk-olympians-compete-saturday-in-rio.aspx

Lair, K. (2016, June 13). Olympics: Meb Keflezighi will try to become oldest marathon medalist. *Los Angeles Daily News.* Retrieved from http://www.dailynews.com/events/20160613/olympics-meb-keflezighi-will-try-to-become-oldest-marathon-medalist

Lambert, J. (2016, June 28). Sydney McLaughlin got the biggest shock of her life from one of the world's biggest stars. *NJ.com.* Retrieved from http://highschoolsports.nj.com/news/article/3644421046326905892/sydney-mclaughlin-of-union-catholic-named-girls-gatorade-national-track-and-field-athlete-of-year/

Lancaster, M. (2016, August 17). Rio Olympics 2016: Americans Tianna Bartoletta, Brittney Reese go 1-2 in long jump. *Sporting News.* Retrieved from http://www.sportingnews.com/athletics/news/rio-olympics-2016-tianna-bartoletta-brittney-reese-long-jump-gold-silver-medals/tbp8mubx26jy1e8kvvgruwgos

Lancaster, M. (2016, August 17). Rio Olympics 2016: Americans Tianna Bartoletta, Brittney Reese go 1-2 in long jump. *SportingNews.* Retrieved from http://www.sportingnews.com/athletics/news/rio-olympics-2016-tianna-bartoletta-brittney-reese-long-jump-gold-silver-medals/tbp8mubx26jy1e8kvvgruwgos

Layden, T. (2016, August 15). Usain Bolt provides moment of pleasure for track and field, Olympics with 100m gold. *Sports Illustrated.* Retrieved from http://www.si.com/olympics/2016/08/15/usain-bolt-100m-gold-medal-rio-olympics-justin-gatlin

Layden, T. (2016, August 17). U.S.'s Jenny Simpson won't let half-empty Rio stadium dull historic Olympic moment. *Sports Illustrated.* Retrieved from http://www.si.com/olympics/2016/08/17/jenny-simpson-bronze-1500m-rio-olympic-stadium-empty

Layden, T. (2016, July 3). Tori Bowie ready to make her case as the next great U.S. women's sprinter. *Sports Illustrated.* Retrieved from http://www.si.com/olympics/2016/07/02/rio-olympics-us-track-and-field-trials-tori-bowie

Lee, J. (2016, July 8). Usain Bolt named to Olympic team despite injuries at trials. *The Washington Post.* Retrieved from https://www.washingtonpost.com/news/early-lead/wp/2016/07/08/usain-bolt-named-to-olympic-team-despite-injuries-at-trials/

Leith, W. (2016, July 16). Greg Rutherford: welcome to my life. *The Times.* Retrieved from http://www.thetimes.co.uk/article/greg-rutherford-welcome-to-my-life-9qmrvf7t0

LetsRun.com. (2016, August 11). Men's pole vault preview: Will Renaud Lavillenie become the first man in 60 years to repeat as Olympic champion? Retrieved from http://www.letsrun.com/news/2016/08/mens-pole-vault-preview-will-renaud-lavillenie-become-first-man-60-years-repeat-olympic-champion/

LetsRun.com. (2016, July 1). 2016 Olympic Trials begin with chaos – Donavan Brazier and Duane Solomon bomb out in 1st round of men's 800. Retrieved from http://www.letsrun.com/news/2016/07/2016-olympic-trials-begin-chaos-donavan-brazier-duane-solomon-bomb-1st-round-mens-800/

LetsRun.com. (2016, July 14). Mason Finley – US Olympic Trials discus champion – Credits much of success to the fact he's lost 87 pounds, says cardio work and nutrition are the keys to massive weight loss. Retrieved from http://www.letsrun.com/news/2016/07/mason-finley-us-olympic-trials-discus-champion-credits-much-success-fact-hes-lost-87-pounds-says-cardio-work-nutrition-keys-massive-weight-loss/

LetsRun.com. (2016, July 8). 11 minutes with Evan Jager after he wins Olympic Trials and his 5th straight USATF crown. Retrieved from http://www.letsrun.com/news/2016/07/11-minutes-evan-jager-wins-olympic-trials-5th-straight-usatf-crown/

Levine, D. (2016, August 17). Kristi Castlin: 5 fast facts you need to know. *Heavy.* Retrieved from http://heavy.com/sports/2016/08/kristi-castlin-father-murdered-bio-who-is-track-and-field-hurdler-100m-rio-olympics-bindi/

Levine, D. (2016, August 19). Dalilah Muhammad: 5 fast facts you need to know. *Heavy.* Retrieved from http://heavy.com/sports/2016/08/dalilah-muhammad-400-meter-hurdles-who-is-bio-favorite-stats-team-usa-rio-olympics-track-family-religion/

Loh, S. (2016, July 3). Jeremy Taiwo wins silver medal at U.S. Olympic trials to advance to his first Olympic Games. *The Seattle Times.* Retrieved from http://www.seattletimes.com/sports/olympics/jeremy-taiwo-wins-silver-medal-at-u-s-olympic-trials-to-advance-to-his-first-olympic-games/

Longman, J. (2016, August 14). Usain Bolt is still the world's fastest man. *The New York Times.* Retrieved from http://www.nytimes.com/2016/08/15/sports/olympics/usain-bolt-100-meters-justin-gatlin-results.html

Longman, J. (2016, August 21). How Matt Centrowitz won a historic 1,500 meters. *The New York Times.* Retrieved from http://www.nytimes.com/2016/08/22/sports/olympics/matt-centrowitz-won-1500-meters-metric-mile.html?_r=0

Longman, J. (2016, July 4). Runner Boris Berian goes from McDonald's employee to a symbol of athletes' rights. *The New York Times.* Retrieved from http://www.nytimes.com/2016/07/05/sports/olympics/runner-boris-berian-goes-from-mcdonalds-employee-to-a-symbol-of-athletes-rights.html

Maese, R. (2016, August 17). American Evan Jager keeps cool and calmly collects silver in the steeplechase. *The Washington Post.* Retrieved from https://www.washingtonpost.com/sports/olympics/american-evan-jager-keeps-cool-and-calmly-collects-silver-in-the-steeplechase/2016/08/17/d9f78528-6493-11e6-be4e-23fc4d4d12b4_story.html

Maese, R. (2016, August 19). Chaunté Lowe, her priorities in order, hopes to high-jump to the medal stand. *The Washington Post.* Retrieved from https://www.washingtonpost.com/sports/olympics/chaunte-lowe-her-priorities-in-order-hopes-to-high-jump-to-the-medal-stand/2016/08/19/4932b05e-6613-11e6-8b27-bb8ba39497a2_story.html

Maese, R. (2016, July 26). 16-year-old Sydney McLaughlin juggles Olympics, school—and juggling. *The Washington Post.* Retrieved from https://www.washingtonpost.com/sports/olympics/16-year-old-sydney-mclaughlin-juggles-olympics-school--and-juggling/2016/07/26/af10b41e-502b-11e6-a7d8-13d06b37f256_story.html

Maese, R. (2016, July 3). Vashti Cunningham finishes second in high jump to claim spot on U.S. Olympic team. *Washington Post.* Retrieved from https://www.washingtonpost.com/sports/vashti-cunningham-finishes-second-in-high-jump-to-claim-spot-on-us-olympic-team/2016/07/03/57c79b98-4188-11e6-88d0-6adee48be8bc_story.html

Makin, C. (2016, July 21). Sydney McLaughlin is off and running—to Rio. *myCentralJersey.com.* Retrieved from http://www.mycentraljersey.com/story/sports/olympics/rio-2016/2016/07/20/sydney-mclaughlin-off-and-running-rio/87282228/

Malle, C. (2016, March 31). Meet the Dibabas: The fastest family on the planet. *Vogue.* Retrieved from http://www.vogue.com/13419749/dibaba-family-ethiopian-distance-runners-olympics-2016-rio-de-janeiro/

Marathon Meb. (2016). Retrieved from https://marathonmeb.com/meb-keflezighi/

McQuade, A. (2016, August 14). UGA's Keturah Orji sets new American record in triple jump. *WXIA-TV.* Retrieved from http://www.11alive.com/sports/olympics/georgia-athletes/ugas-keturah-orji-sets-new-american-record-in-triple-jump/297481621

Meyer, J. (2016, August 15). Boris Berian finishes eighth in 800-meter final. *The Denver Post.* Retrieved from http://www.denverpost.com/2016/08/15/boris-berian-finishes-eighth-in-800-meter-final/

Meyer, J. (2016, August 16). Janay DeLoach, Kara Winger both barely miss qualifying in their field events at Rio Olympics. *The Denver Post.* Retrieved from http://www.denverpost.com/2016/08/16/janay-deloach-kara-winger-miss-qualifying-rio-olympics/

Miller, J. (2016, August 11). From 1:54 to 1:44: The meteoric rise of Clayton Murphy. *FloTrack.* Retrieved from http://www.flotrack.org/article/44897-from-1-54-to-1-44-the-meteoric-rise-of-clayton-murphy

Milles, T. (2016, July 29). Best way to prepare for the Olympics? Train with teenagers. *The News Tribune.* Retrieved from http://www.thenewstribune.com/sports/olympics/article92787522.html#storylink=cpy

Morrison, A. (2016, July 24). Hometown hero. *The Toledo Blade.* Retrieved from http://www.toledoblade.com/Editorials/2016/07/24/Hometown-hero.html

Myerberg, P. (2016, August 11). Mental approach changed, injuries healed, Brittney Reese eyes repeat. *USA Today.* Retrieved from http://www.usatoday.com/story/sports/olympics/rio-2016/2016/08/11/britney-reese-

Myerberg, P. (2016, August 21). Bronze medalist Galen Rupp on the marathon: 'Maybe this is my best event.' *USA Today.* Retrieved from http://www.usatoday.com/story/sports/olympics/rio-2016/2016/08/21/galen-rupp-olympic-marathon-bronze-medal/89077806/

Myerberg, P. (2016, May 29). 40-year-old sprinter Kim Collins shares secret to longevity. *USA Today.* Retrieved from http://www.usatoday.com/story/sports/olympics/rio-2016/2016/05/24/40-year-old-sprinter-kim-collins-shares-secret-longevity/84854860/

Nayyar, N. (2016, January 11). Brittney Reese: Olympic champion and five time world champion in long jump reveals her success mantra "You don't have to be great to start but you have to start to be great." *Women Fitness.* Retrieved from http://www.womenfitness.net/brittney-reese.htm

Nexstar Broadcasting, Inc. (2016, May 29). Sandi Morris injury wrist in pole break. Retrieved from http://www.nwahomepage.com/razorback-nation/sandi-morris-injury-wrist-in-pole-break

O'Neill, P. (2016, July 9). *TwinCities.com Pioneer Press.* Retrieved from http://www.twincities.com/2016/07/09/olympic-track-trials-ex-gopher-hassan-mead-qualifies-for-rio-in-5000/

Odom, J. (2016, August 18). Ashton Eaton wins decathlon gold in Rio: Event results at 2016 Olympics. *Oregon Live.* Retrieved from http://www.oregonlive.com/olympics/index.ssf/2016/08/ashton_eaton_decathlon_schedul.html

Oestreich, A. (2016, August 1). Double trouble? Ankle injury has Allyson Felix on edge for trials. *FloTrack*. Retrieved from http://www.flotrack.org/article/43178-double-trouble-ankle-injury-has-allyson-felix-on-edge-for-trials

Oestreich, A. (2016, February 12). Interview with Amy Hastings Cragg. *FloTrack*. Retrieved from http://www.flotrack.org/article/39613-interview-with-amy-hastings-cragg

Omaha World-Herald. (2016, July 9). Nebraska native Maggie Malone makes Olympic team. Retrieved from http://www.omaha.com/sports/local-sports/nebraska-native-maggie-malone-makes-olympic-team/article_b0888af2-4657-11e6-8724-83074179144c.html

Parker, M. (2016, August 5). Galen Rupp, Olympic runner: 5 fast facts you need to know. *Heavy*. Retrieved from http://heavy.com/sports/2016/08/galen-rupp-olympic-runner-5-fast-facts-you-need-to-know-track-and-field-rio-2016-competing-athletes-marathon/

Pepin, M. (2016, August 17). Abbey D'Agostino won't be able to run in 5,000 final. *Boston Globe*. Retrieved from https://www.bostonglobe.com/sports/olympics2016/2016/08/17/abbey-agostino-won-able-run-final/CWDO0QnWLNopWqBZqh558L/story.html

Peters, C. (2016, August 19). Rio Olympics: Ashton Eaton cements legacy with second decathlon gold medal. *CBS Sports*. Retrieved from http://www.cbssports.com/olympics/news/rio-olympics-ashton-eaton-cements-legacy-with-second-decathlon-gold-medal/

Phillips, M. (2016, August 15). The toughest fighter' Wayde van Niekerk was fast from the start … he was born 11 weeks early, says gold medalist's mum. *The Sun*. Retrieved from https://www.thesun.co.uk/sport/1617149/wayde-van-niekerk-was-fast-from-the-start-he-was-born-11-weeks-early-says-gold-medallists-mum/

Pilkington, C. (2016, March 2). 10 moments that shaped Shalane Flanagan's life. *Women's Running*. Retrieved from http://womensrunning.competitor.com/2015/04/inspiration/10-moments-that-shaped-shalane-flanagans-life_37407/5#JJoX7LiLTCIblcic.99

Powell, M. (2016, August 18). The Olympics are the end of a track from poverty. *The New York Times*. Retrieved from http://www.nytimes.com/2016/08/19/sports/olympics/high-jumper-chaunte-lowe-road-out-of-poverty.html?_r=0

Ramsak, B. (2012, August 6). London 2012-Event report-Women's 1500m heats. *IAAF*. Retrieved from https://www.iaaf.org/news/report/london-2012-event-report-womens-1500m-hea

Redbook. (2016, July 28). Michelle Carter is the body positive champion we can't wait to see in Rio. Retrieved from http://www.redbookmag.com/body/mental-health/a45271/michelle-carter-body-olympics/

Reid, S. (2011, April 30). USC hurdler Ali learning how to overcome tragedy. *The Orange County Register*. Retrieved from http://www.ocregister.com/articles/angeles-298625-hurdler-learning.html

Reid, S. (2016, July 5). Boris Berian, Charles Jock complete unlikely journeys to U.S. Olympic track team. *The Orange County Register*. Retrieved from http://www.ocregister.com/articles/jock-721500-team-charles.html

Reid, S. (2016, May 27). Road to Rio: From lowest of depths, 800-meter runner Boris Berian now hitting his peak. *The Orange County Register*. Retrieved from http://www.ocregister.com/articles/berian-717500-handler-nike.html

Rice, S. (2016, August 15). Jarrion Lawson loses gold medal due to finger tip in long jump at Rio Olympic. *Business 2 Community*. Retrieved from http://www.business2community.com/sports/jarrion-lawson-loses-gold-medal-due-finger-tip-long-jump-rio-olympics-01626574#5sh6YCLuz3ufbcq7.97

Robertson, L. (2016, August 18). Miami hurdler Brianna Rollins wins Olympic gold, makes her high school coach proud. *Miami Herald*. Retrieved from http://www.miamiherald.com/sports/olympics/article96369437.html#storylink=cpy

Rosen, K. (2016, August 15). Clayton Murphy ends 24-year medal drought in 800-meter. *Team USA*. Retrieved from http://www.teamusa.org/News/2016/August/15/Clayton-Murphy-Ends-24-Year-Medal-Drought-In-800-Meter

Rosen, K. (2016, July 2). Ryan Crouser follows uncle onto Olympic team with monster shot put throw. *Team USA*. Retrieved from http://www.teamusa.org/News/2016/July/02/Ryan-Crouser-Follows-Uncle-Onto-Olympic-Team-With-Monster-Shot-Put-Throw

Rosser, E. (2016). Out of nowhere. *SportsNet.* Retrieved from http://www.sportsnet.ca/olympics/andre-de-grasse-fast-tracked-100-metre-sprint/

Rubinroit, S. (2016, August 10). Three facts you didn't know about the Usain Bolt-Justin Gatlin rivalry. *NBC Olympics.* Retrieved from http://www.nbcolympics.com/news/three-facts-you-didnt-know-about-usain-bolt-justin-gatlin-rivalry

Rubinroit, S. (2016, August 18). Nia Ali's son steals the show. *NBC Olympics.* Retrieved from http://www.nbcolympics.com/news/nia-alis-son-steals-show-rio

Rubinroit, S. (2016, July 10). Brenda Martinez's emotional week at Olympic Trials ends in triumph. *NBC Olympics.* Retrieved from http://www.nbcolympics.com/news/brenda-martinezs-emotional-week-olympic-trials-ends-triumph

Rubinroit, S. (2016, July 13). The Olympic gold medalist who appeared in a Beyoncé music video. *NBC Olympics.* Retrieved from http://www.nbcolympics.com/news/olympic-gold-medalist-who-appeared-beyonce-music-video

Run Blog Run. (2015, December 13). The spin on the throw princess, Aggie's Shelbi Vaughan is already discus royalty. Retrieved from http://www.runblogrun.com/2015/12/the-spin-on-the-throw-princess-aggies-shelbi-vaughan-is-already-discus-royalty.html

Sada, M. (2016, August 11). Rio 2016: Latina track star Brenda Martinez defeats all odds in pursuit of her Olympic career. *Fox News Latino.* Retrieved from http://latino.foxnews.com/latino/sports/2016/08/11/latina-track-star-defeats-all-odds-in-pursuit-her-olympic-career/

Schnell, L. (2016, August 11). A long run back: How English Gardner overcame depression, anxiety on road to Rio. *Sports Illustrated.* Retrieved from http://www.si.com/olympics/2016/08/11/english-gardner-rio-olympics-track-and-field-depression-anxiety

Sebor, J. (2016, July 11). Meet the 16-year-old who just made the Olympic team. *Women's Running.* Retrieved from http://womensrunning.competitor.com/2016/07/news/meet-16-year-old-phenom-just-made-olympic-team_62108

Sherrington, K. (2016, August 15). Texas A&M's Shelbi Vaughan calls Olympics 'an amazing experience' despite tough finish; Bahamas' Shaunae Miller lays out for gold. *SportsDay.* Retrieved from http://sportsday.dallasnews.com/other-sports/olympics/2016/08/15/shelbi-vaughan-calls-olympics-amazing-experience-despite-tough-finish-bahamas-shaunae-miller-lays-gold

Sherrington, K. (2016, August 18). Texan hurdler Kerron Clement finally nabs gold, has message for Olympic dopers. *SportsDay.* Retrieved from http://sportsday.dallasnews.com/othersports/olympics/2016/08/18/texankerron-clement-captures-olympic-gold-400-meter-hurdles

Slocum, M. (2016, July 6). USOC dampens Kate Grace's victory by forcing her sponsor, Oiselle, to take down images over trademark issue. *The Orange County Register.* Retrieved from http://www.ocregister.com/articles/athletes-721741-olympic-usoc.html

Spikes. (2013, December 4). Why, why, why Dalilah? Retrieved from https://spikes.iaaf.org/post/why-why-why-dalilah

Spikes. (2014, September 8). I'm a survivor. Retrieved from https://spikes.iaaf.org/post/novlene-williams-mills-breast-cancer-survivor

Sprunk, C. (2016, April 22). Olympic Track and Field hopeful English Gardner has an alter ego named 'Baby Beast.' *US Weekly.* http://www.usmagazine.com/celebrity-news/news/olympic-hopeful-english-gardner-on-her-alter-ego-baby-beast-w203846

Stevens, A. (2016, July 20). The final hurdle: With tragic past behind, Castlin eyes Olympic medal. *myAJC.* Retrieved from http://www.myajc.com/news/news/local/the-final-hurdle-with-tragic-past-behind-castlin-e/nr2pH/

Strout, E. (2016, August 13). Galen Rupp: "You gotta have a short memory in this sport sometimes." *Runner's World.* Retrieved from http://www.runnersworld.com/olympics/galen-rupp-you-gotta-have-a-short-memory-in-this-sport-sometimes

Strout, E. (2016, August 15). Emma Coburn wins first-ever U.S. medal in women's steeplechase. *Runner's World.* Retrieved from http://www.runnersworld.com/olympics/emma-coburn-wins-first-ever-us-medal-in-womens-steeplechase

Strout, E. (2016, February 1). Marathon training is a team effort for Flanagan and Cragg. *Runner's World*. Retrieved from http://www.runnersworld.com/olympic-trials/marathon-training-is-a-team-effort-for-flanagan-and-cragg

Stubbs, R. (2016, August 13). Jeff Henderson wins first U.S. long jump gold medal since 2004; Jarrion Lawson comes in a controversial fourth place. *The Washington Post*. Retrieved from https://www.washingtonpost.com/olympics/2016/live-updates/rio-games/scores-and-latest-news/jeff-henderson-wins-first-u-s-long-jump-gold-medal-since-2004-jarrion-lawson-comes-in-a-controversial-fourth-place/

Sun Herald. (2016, July 1). 2016 Olympic hopeful Brittney Reese already golden. Retrieved from http://www.sunherald.com/opinion/editorials/article87044437.html

Svrluga, B. (2016, August 21). Galen Rupp takes marathon bronze, capping a U.S. distance running resurgence. *The Washington Post*. Retrieved from https://www.washingtonpost.com/sports/olympics/galen-rupp-takes-marathon-bronze-capping-a-us-distance-running-resurgence/2016/08/21/84732db8-67a0-11e6-ba32-5a4bf5aad4fa_story.html

Tadias Magazine. (2016, August 17). Rio 2016 Olympics: Genzebe Dibaba takes silver medal in the women's 1,500 meters. http://www.tadias.com/08/17/2016/rio-2016-olympics-genzebe-dibaba-takes-silver-medal-in-the-womens-1500-meters/

Tatyana McFadden. (2016). About Tatyanna. Retrieved from http://tatyanamcfadden.com/about-tatyana/

Texas A&M University. (2016, July 2). Texas A&M's Shelbi Vaughan earns Olympic Trials discus silver to secure trip to Rio. Retrieved from http://12thman.com/news/2016/7/2/track-and-field-texas-ams-shelbi-vaughan-earns-olympic-trials-discus-silver-to-secure-trip-to-rio.aspx

Texas A&M University. (2016, June 9). Collegiate javelin record for Maggie Malone, NCAA decathlon title for Lindon Victor. Retrieved from http://12thman.com/news/2016/6/9/track-and-field-collegiate-javelin-record-for-maggie-malone-ncaa-decathlon-title-for-lindon-victor.aspx

University of Colorado. (n.d.). Roster. Retrieved from http://www.cubuffs.com/roster.aspx?rp_

USA Today Sports. (2016, July 10). Bernard Lagat, at 41, wins 5,000 to qualify for his fifth Olympics. Retrieved from http://www.usatoday.com/story/sports/olympics/rio-2016/2016/07/09/us-olympic-trials-bernard-lagat-aries-merritt/86907800/

USA Today Sports. (2016, July 9). Justin Gatlin wins 200 title at U.S. Olympic trials. Retrieved from http://www.usatoday.com/story/sports/olympics/rio-2016/2016/07/09/us-olympic-trials-200-final-justin-gatlin-lashawn-merritt/86907698/

USA Track and Field. (n.d.). Athlete Bios. Retrieved http://www.usatf.org/Athlete-Bios/Nia-Ali.aspx

USADA. (2016, June 13). U.S. Track & Field athlete, Berry, accepts sanction for rule violation. Retrieved from http://www.usada.org/gwen-berry-accepts-sanction/

Vegun, D. (2016, July 7). Soldier vaults to US Olympic team, breaks trial record. *U.S. Army*. Retrieved from https://www.army.mil/article/171175/soldier_vaults_to_us_olympic_team_breaks_trial_record

Verry, P. (2016, July 19). American Olympians to watch in Rio: Runner Jenny Simpson. *Footwear News*. Retrieved from http://footwearnews.com/2016/focus/athletic-outdoor/usa-olympic-athletes-to-watch-rio-runner-jenny-simpson-241079/

Walsh, S. (2016, August 13). Tori Bowie: 5 fast facts you need to know. *Heavy*. Retrieved from http://heavy.com/sports/2016/08/tori-bowie-runner-instagram-photos-pics-2016-track-field-rio-olympics/

Wanja, C. (2016, July 15). Yego ready to break pain barrier for Olympics glory. *Citizen Digital*. Retrieved from http://citizentv.co.ke/sports/yego-ready-to-break-pain-barrier-for-olympics-glory-133654/

Washington, J. (2016, August 15). Justin Gatlin can't outrun Usain Bolt, doping past. *ESPN*. Retrieved from http://www.espn.com/olympics/trackandfield/story/_/id/17306390/olympics-2016-justin-gatlin-outrun-usain-bolt-doping-past

Washington, J. (2016, July 4). High-jumper Chaunte Lowe not ceding to the future just yet. *ESPN*. Retrieved from http://espn.go.com/olympics/trackandfield/story/_/id/16750262/olympic-track-trials-2016-high-jumper-chaunte-lowe-not-ceding-future-just-yet

Washington, J. (2016, July 4). High-jumper Chaunte Lowe not ceding to the future just yet. *ESPN*. Retrieved from http://www.espn.com/olympics/trackandfield/story/_/id/16750262/olympic-track-trials-2016-high-jumper-chaunte-lowe-not-ceding-future-just-yet

Whiteside, K. (2016, September 1). A Paralympian races to remove obstacles for the next generation. *The New York Times*. Retrieved from http://www.nytimes.com/2016/09/04/sports/olympics/paralympics-tatyana-mcfadden-wheelchair.html?_r=0

Williams, C. (2016, August 14). Former TCU sprinter Kim Collins ready to retire soon after Olympics. *Star-Telegram*. Retrieved from http://www.star-telegram.com/sports/olympics/article9568 4652.html#storylink=cpy

Williams, C. (2016, August 15). A&M discus thrower Shelbi Vaughan cherishes Olympic experience. *Star-Telegram*. Retrieved from http://www.star-telegram.com/sports/olympics/article9587 8537.html#storylink=cpy

Williams, M. (2016, July 11). Topsfield's D'Agostino headed to Rio for Olympics after 5th place finish. *The Salem News*. Retrieved from http://www.salemnews.com/sports/updated-topsfield-s-d-agostino-headed-to-rio-for-olympics/article_7577bd64-79d6-58ed-8b9a-7a351536ff49.html

Woody, D. (2016, June 26). Leap of faith: Olympic medalist DeLoach puts right leg forward. *Alaska Dispatch Publishing*. Retrieved from http://www.adn.com/sports/2016/06/26/leap-of-faith-olympic-medalist-deloach-puts-right-leg-forward/

WSB-TV Atlanta. (2016, June 13). Georgia's Keturah Orji shatters NCAA, American records for triple jump title. Retrieved from http://www.wsbtv.com/sports/college/university-of-georgia/georgias-keturah-orji-shatters-ncaa-american-records-for-triple-jump-title/340500027

Yale University Athletics. (2016, July 4). Kate Grace '11 earns spot on team USA at Rio Olympics. Retrieved from http://www.yalebulldogs.com/sports/w-track/2016-17/releases/20160704y 1cb11

Young, D. (2016, July 11). Matt Centrowitz is too good, Andrews and Blankenship stop Manzano's streak. *FloTrack*. Retrieved from http://www.flotrack.org/article/43478-matt-centrowitz-is-too-good-andrews-and-blankenship-stop-manzano-s-streak

Zaccardi, N, (2016, September 18). Tatyana McFadden upset in Rio Paralympic marathon, finishes with historic medal haul. *NBC Sports*. Retrieved from http://olympics.nbcsports.com/2016/09/18/tatyana-mcfadden-paralympics-marathon-rio/

Zaccardi, N. (2015, June 24). Joe Kovacs' emergence from family tragedy, Olympic miss to world leader. *NBC Sports*. Retrieved from http://olympics.nbcsports.com/2015/06/24/joe-kovacs-shot-put-usa-track-and-field-championships/

Zaccardi, N. (2016, February 8). Ajeé Wilson learned from sitting out World Championships. *NBC Sports*. Retrieved from http://olympics.nbcsports.com/2016/02/08/ajee-wilson-injury-track-and-field-800-meters-olympics/

Zaccardi, N. (2016, June 24). Joe Kovacs' emergence from family tragedy, Olympic miss to world leader. *NBC Sports*. Retrieved from http://olympics.nbcsports.com/2015/06/24/joe-kovacs-shot-put-usa-track-and-field-championships/

Zahn, J. (2016). Dalilah Muhammad overcomes adversity one hurdle at a time. *FloSports*. Retrieved from http://featured.flosports.tv/dalilah-muhammad-overcomes-obstacles-to-become-favorite-for-gold

Zeigler, M. (2016, August 20). Las Vegan Vashti Cunningham fails to medal in Olympic high jump. *Review Journal*. Retrieved from http://www.reviewjournal.com/sports/olympics/las-vegan-vashti-cunningham-fails-medal-olympic-high-jump

Zillgitt, J. (2016, August 15). Clayton Murphy earns the USA's first medal in the 800 since 1992. *USA Today*. Retrieved from http://www.usatoday.com/story/sports/olympics/rio-2016/2016/08/15/clayton-murphy-800-meters-bronze-medal/88814806/

About the Authors

Dr. Mark Stanbrough is a professor in the Department of Health, Physical Education and Recreation at Emporia State University in Kansas. He teaches graduate and undergraduate exercise physiology and sports psychology classes and is the director of Coaching Education. The Coaching Education program at Emporia State is currently one of only ten universities in the United State to be accredited by the National Council for the Accreditation of Coaching Education. He was a co-founder of the online physical education graduate program, the first in the United States to go completely online. He received his Ph.D. in exercise physiology from the University of Oregon, and undergraduate and master's degrees from Emporia State in physical education. He has served as department chair and has served on the National Association for Sport and Physical Education National Sport Steering Committee and is a past member of the board of directors for the National Council for the Accreditation of Coaching Education.

Mark has over thirty years of coaching experience at the collegiate, high school, middle school and club level. Coach Stanbrough served eight years as the head men's and women's cross country/track and field coach at Emporia State (1984-1992) with the 1986 women's cross country team finishing second at the NAIA national meet. He has also coached at Emporia High School and Glasco High School in Kansas. He is a member of the Emporia State University Athletic Hall of Honor and the Health, Physical Education, Recreation Hall of Honor and has won numerous coach-of-the-year awards at the high school and collegiate levels. Mark is a past USATF Association president and has served as head referee at numerous national track and field/cross country competitions.

Jenna Hill holds a Masters of Science degree in Instructional Design and Technology from Emporia State University and a Bachelor of Arts degree in Mass Media from Baker University.

She was named to the Baker University Dean's List, was a member of National Society of Collegiate Scholars, and a member of Alpha Delta Sigma Honor Society. She was an editor for The Baker Orange newspaper for three years and was honored for her work by the Kansas Associated Collegiate Press and the Associated Collegiate Press. She was named the Instructional Design and Technology Outstanding Graduate Student of the Year and was vice president of the Emporia State University Instructional Design and Technology Student Association.

Jenna has been involved with the sport of track and field from the age of 6, when she competed in age group track and field for Emporia High School. She went on to compete in track and field and cross country for Baker University, where she was a multiple-time Heart of American Conference individual champion and was part of seven conference championship teams including cross country, indoor, and outdoor track and field. She is also a member of the school record holding 4x400 meter team. She continues to compete in road races, and finished her first marathon in the spring of 2016, along with several half marathon finishes. She also worked as a cross country coach at Andover High School. She is currently an editor for Roho Publishing.